52 Pick Me Up

Pamela Aloia

March Baby Publishing
Second Edition 2012

Additional copies are available at www.solangel.com
Library of Congress Control Number: 2012910199
ISBN: 978-0-578-10802-5

Editor: Macrina Russo
Illustrations: Michael Aloia
Layout & Cover Design: A Creation Productions www.acreations.com

For more information:
Sol Angel
Pamela Aloia
Po Box 26452
Collegeville, PA 19426
www.solangel.com

Printed in the USA

Acknowledgements

Mary, Dutch, Isaac, Sara, John Michael, Joy, and Jasmine, each who have played a significant role in opening my heart to perceiving my Truth.

My heartfelt gratitude to Michael, for his endless love and support;
Antonio and Annelise, for their continued guidance and lessons;
Mom, Dad, Ralph, and Gina for helping shape the person I am today;
My teachers, mentors, students, clients who have walked in and out of my life, for their achievements and character have inspired me to continue walking my path.

Contents

Preface

I started these writings as a tool to help myself become more aware – spiritually aware at first, but the more I worked with the writings, the more I learned to change my beliefs, my mental state of a specific situation, and then move from there. I believe our thoughts do really create our reality. What we think and what we believe really is what our expectations become, and, therefore, our experiences. The more we can tailor our minds to bring forth that which we ultimately desire for the good of us and the good of those around us, the happier our lives are, and the lives we touch along the way.

This book is about finding conscious awareness in all we do. Sure it takes time, and it takes effort, but it's not as difficult as most people think. The awareness part is simple; the more challenging part is making the change. Once we understand the mentality or the emotions behind the actions and reactions, the sooner we are able to find a response that works best for us and that works best for where we are at this moment.

For a long time, I suppressed my innermost thoughts and feelings. I was raised with the practice that you didn't show any internal battles or forlorn, upsetting emotion. On the surface, everything had to be acceptable and easy for others – what I felt inside was secondary. All negative emotions were sent down to the bowels of my being usually to not be addressed ever, or worse, to be released in an outrage that seemed inappropriate at the time.

At a physically unhealthy time in my life, I sought therapy and learned that I was not doing a good job of expressing my feelings. With time, I learned that I could speak about my likes and dislikes and voice my frustrations about life. This was a wonderful epiphany for me. I cannot tell you how much the love and experiences of my relationships have grown and changed in ways I never imagined possible over the years simply due to open communication. My sense of humor has expanded immensely and I love to laugh a whole lot, especially during frustrating times. My husband and I support each other and our goals with amazing grace and passion, leaving room for down time, leisure activities, and discussion. All this is true because we were able to become more aware of who we are at each given moment.

As I've become more aware and in tune with my own well being, all my relationships have changed – those with my children, extended family, and co-workers. Life seems more productive, fruitful, and a bit more at ease.

52 Pick Me Up offers you an easy-to-use, simple-to-gain-results method of becoming aware of you. In becoming aware of you, you become more understanding of yourself. You even become more understanding and tolerant of others' reactions, including your own.

A plentiful helping of compassion for yourself is needed for this journey. As you travel this journey you'll identify and start to let go of expectations and judgments of who you are and how you should act. You start to open your eyes and heart to inner and expressed freedom to be a loving, compassionate, sovereign you.

Energy Awareness

All things are energy. Everything emits some type of energy – people emit energy, furniture, trees, rocks, cars, etc., everything is made up of energy. Therefore, it's not so far fetched to understand that our thoughts and our words have energy. You know what it feels like too – you know what it feels like when you've been around a TV or computer or phone equipment for extended amounts of time, or if you get drained from shopping, or if you feel relaxed around a specific group of people – your energy is being altered simply by your surroundings.

Consciously or subconsciously, our bodies are affected by the energy around us. Whether it's electromagnetic waves or negative thoughts and emotions from those around us, our physical, emotional, mental and spiritual bodies are weakened or strengthened by what surrounds us as well as by our learned reactions to our environment.

There are many classes available to the public that teach tools to help understand and be more aware of the energy around us – including our own energy. Being aware of this energy is extremely helpful when it comes to living in the flow. Energy awareness helps heighten our ability to be the flow.

Energy awareness is simply tapping into the unseen waves of thoughts and actions that pervade a person or situation's space. Many of us are in tune with energy without the need of formal training. For some, formal training does provide many tools with which to harness and spread loving energy. Formal energetic awareness can also help ease an acceptance of certain situations. Energy awareness helps bridge the gap between what we think is going on to what we know is truly happening.

There are many types and levels of energy awareness for wherever your comfort zone resides. Energy awareness can be as simple as tapping into our own feelings or someone else's rather than solely looking at what's stated on the surface. It can also be as complicated as learning a new technique or signing up for a class to learn a specific type of energy recognition and/or healing. There are various types of Reiki available as well as a myriad of other energy modalities that seem to heighten our awareness of good in our world. Each modality generally provides tools to help us move along our own path as well as help others down theirs.

Someone is always in need of help and someone is always available to help us if we take a moment and feel the appropriate avenues. In a society where what we do far outweighs our expectation to be who we are, taking time to feel what we're feeling can seem to be an inconvenience, especially at first. Many of us know how to hide emotions even from ourselves. So opening up to ourselves first can be scary and an unknown. It can also be quite liberating. Once we allow ourselves the emotional exploration tempered with detached mental objectivity, we are on the pathway to an easier life.

Becoming aware of the energies we emit, we can learn how our energy seems to compliment the energies around us. We can determine what potential external factors affect our energy in positive or not so positive ways. Being in tune with our mental and emotional selves serves as an effective type of energy awareness.

Through using this book you will become more aware of yourselves, people, places, objects, etc,

and your initial response to them. Cherish each
moment, for they are filled with opportunities.

Ordinary can be Extraordinary

I was working long hours at a high-energy corporate job, raising two young children and managing
their activities. My husband was working long con-
tractor hours, and playing in a band a few nights a
week – we were constantly on the go. As a result of
the many stresses, my health began to decline. My
main issue became migraines - daily migraines, migraines that would last 3-5 days, and migraines
that intensified with any type of physical activity.
Growing up as an athlete I found my only outlet of
exercise no longer an option. I became distraught
and withdrawn.

The pain was constant. The medical field pre-
scribed medication after medication. Some worked;
some didn't; some worked for a while then stopped.
I could feel my spirit dwindling. Daily medication
made it possible for me to muster up the energy to
attend my work day, muddle through it somehow,
come home and lie on the couch or in bed. I really
don't know how my family lived with me during that
time. I found little pleasure in anything I did and

resorted to hibernation whenever possible as a means to deal with the pain. When I did venture out people would ask why I was squinting – I didn't even realize that squinting was my involuntary reaction of dealing with the pain.

My husband had accompanied me to various places of alternative therapy options – chiropractor, acupuncture, kinesiology, cranio-sacral massage, etc. We lost count of how much money we spent and how far we traveled at the recommendation from any person who sparked a remote sense of hope for a possible respite from the pain. I changed my diet, the way I slept, how I exercised.

The side effects of one of my medications were more than I was willing to endure any longer, so I decided one morning that I was going off them. I stopped immediately and initially felt a lot of relief from the decision. Then, the fear crept in – the fear of experiencing the intense pain and incapacitation every day. I knew folks at my job were growing weary of my condition, some I'm sure, even thought I was faking it to take time off from work periodically. They had no idea how dire I felt my situation was. Nor could I ever expect them to understand it.

With my resolve to eliminate foreign substances from my body came a push to live. I had not been living for a few years at this point and I began to realize that I needed to live – somehow. I had been off my prescription medications for about two weeks when I signed up for a Reiki I class. We weren't in the position to buy anything except necessities, so this was a big deal to spending $100 on a Reiki class. Reiki had always been something I was interested in, but never took the time or saved the money to take. With a resolve to live, I opted to take Reiki for the fun of it.

The Reiki class marks the beginning of an era in my life. It's truly the time I started becoming more aware – of everything. My perspectives started changing. I expressed my thoughts and emotions more. I began having tremendously vivid dreams, three or four in a night – and all I wanted to do was practice Reiki any time I could.

The most amazing thing happened about three weeks after taking the class – I realized I was migraine free. The intensity of my headaches decreased significantly and I felt better than I had in years. I traced back the time to when I started feeling better to the day of the Reiki class. Not that Reiki healed me, but my openness to the energy and having no expectations did. Reiki is very powerful – can it help heal everyone? I do believe so. I also believe that some people respond better to one modality better than others. I just happened to respond incredibly well to Reiki.

Since that moment of realization, many years have passed and I have expanded upon my energetic studies, skills, and daily practices. I've made meditation a part of my life. I opened up my own healing center, Sol Angel. I journaled frequently, sometimes reflecting upon life's happenings or observations. Sometimes I would share my writings with my students, clients, and peers. Regularly, I reread my writings, inspired by my observations and interpretations, and supported by consistent, positive comments from my readers.

Despite all the obvious progress and integrated information, I still felt that I needed to slow down. I began to focus on creating something where I could focus on me without setting aside gobs of time to do so. All the self-actualization books I read and all the workshops I attended had an underlying theme of focusing on the necessity of being aware – aware of thoughts that cross our minds, and the emotions we suppress or don't suppress throughout the day.

To help me be more aware I started writing short excerpts on daily events, how I felt about them, and how I could change how I thought and felt about them on the spot. Writing each excerpt was a learning process in and of itself. Implementing them in my weeks was even more rewarding and inspiring. I began to see so much about myself and others that I never saw before – all by changing my awareness and my perspective.

Weekly excerpts provided me a central focus and enough time to integrate what I read. It gave me enough time to be consciously aware to really process and practice what I wanted to incorporate into my life as a whole. Reading the excerpts was quick and simple. I found them easy and effective. I trust they will be for you as well.

How to Use this Book

This book is intended to be read weekly, but you may also randomly open to a page, read an excerpt and go from there. Each excerpt includes common cumbersome situations and then eases you into potentially viewing the situation with a spark of hope or encouraging aspect. Each excerpt challenges you to perceive things differently – some will be easy and others may not be so easy.

To help the awareness factor kick in, each excerpt is accompanied with an exercise and an affirmation. Through the exercises, you can immediately start integrating the awareness into your conscious thoughts. By using the affirmations you solicit the help of your subconscious mind to perceive the world a little differently. My hope is that you will do the associated exercises and say the affirmations regularly throughout your week.

All it takes is just one incident where you see something you didn't quite see before – and you'll feel the difference. It can become a game almost. Initially, you'll see that your reactions are very much in tact. But with practice and awareness, we can all learn to respond – to take the time to acknowledge our feelings, choose our thoughts, and then choose our responses.

Affirmations
An affirmation is a statement asserting the existence or the truth of something.

Affirmations are used in all cultures. They work. Some say that newly introduced affirmations don't work, and to an extent this is true, based on your conscious mind's acceptance of the affirmation. However, your subconscious mind is greatly affected by affirmations even when your conscious mind isn't. Our subconscious accepts what we tell it – regardless what our conscious mind thinks. The more you work with and say or think the affirmation, the more your subconscious is exposed to the words and integrates them on a subconscious level. Eventually, the conscious mind starts picking up on the vibration and accepts the affirmation and the power behind the words as true.

Affirmations are genuinely powerful. There is plenty of documented evidence of people who have survived and surpassed disease and injury through the use of affirmations – to the surprise of many doctors and others.

By using affirmations throughout the week, you'll see how the repetitive information affects you – you may stop a reaction before it happens or gain a better understanding of the reaction after you've experienced it.

Exercises

People learn in all types of different ways – some folks are visual, auditory, experiential or any combination of aspects. By incorporating relative *Reflection Exercises* into your practice, you get to experience what it feels like – what emotions are brought up and why, and then you can determine how to deal with them.

Writing or journaling the exercises can be extremely effective, if you can make the time. Otherwise, taking the time to think through the exercises is a great start.

Kick off

There truly are wonderful layers of exploration within all of us. Awareness can and does change and save lives. Be aware and witness such changes for yourself. Let's get started with changing our lives, one thought at a time!

To the inspired reader:

These writings have been arranged for reference on a weekly basis for a little over a year. How you choose to use them is solely your choice. You may choose to go in order or simply open the book to a page and read the passage you've opened to.

The intent of these writings is to provide something to keep in the back of your mind as you go about your week. The words and thoughts may assist you in being watchful of your own behavior and encourage you to take time to fully understand life's moments for yourself and potentially for others too. As you progress through the year, the hope is for you to acknowledge that which rings true for you and let go of that which does not. Doing so may change your life, introduce a new perspective, and help maintain an open heart.

These writings may also be useful in extracting our personal energetic overlay that keeps us from engaging in the freedom of being our true selves.

May your days and weeks be filled with love, honesty, hope, and joy.
Namaste.

Week 1
Introduction of Self

How we introduce ourselves, the tone in which we speak, the words we choose to use, and the comfort with which we deliver our message plays an important role, not only in how people view us, but more importantly, in how we view ourselves. If we can speak honestly and accurately about who we are, we exude great acceptance of where we are without judgment.

Many corporate executives take time to practice their own introductions. We can do the same. So we are not tongue-tied or so we don't spend a lot of time thinking about how we wish to explain ourselves, it is helpful to rehearse prior to the situation arising. We realize we may wish to introduce ourselves as different roles, since our lives encompass many such roles – work, family, hobbies, etc., yet our roles do not define who we are.

All of our varied roles may define what we do, and yet not necessarily convey who we are at the core. Many of us don't know who we are at the core of our being. We've never been given or possibly taken the opportunity to think about it. People are mostly more concerned with what we do and what we can do for them, than who we are, and how positive we can make each other feel. Because of this, we tend to make what we do more important than who we are, or we directly associate what we do with who we are.

To remove ourselves from this mindset, we can start introducing ourselves by including what we wish people to know about us. Not only will our introduction be unique in that it may include tidbits of information we find fun or important, but since we chose to focus on who we are in our introduction, people will take note of that, and perhaps call upon us for a deeper connection than what was originally anticipated to be experienced.

Of course, a conscious decision must be made to allow those sorts of experiences into our lives. We may be looked upon as odd or eccentric, or we may be welcomed and engaged beyond our expectations. If we are remaining true to ourselves, we give ourselves the power and permission to express ourselves as the beings we are, instead of focusing on the things we do. As a result, our Spirits shine.

Week 1 Reflection Exercise

Take a few moments and consider how you've introduced yourself in the past.

Are you content with the words you use and the overall tone with which you convey words about yourself?

Does your introduction accurately convey what you want it to?

Which aspects of your self introduction are you willing to change so they are more in line with who you are versus who you'd like others to perceive you to be?

How can you change your introduction of self to be more in line with your desires?

You may consider writing down an introduction and working with it until you feel it fits you. Practicing your introduction in the mirror until you are comfortable with it is a useful exercise as well.

Week 1 Affirmation

I am open and confident to share who I am with others.

Week 2
Hammering Home

When we hold a newborn baby or help raise a small child, we tend to project all the important life instructions and lessons we've learned onto that new being. As the child grows, we repeat common lessons and rules in the hopes the child picks up on them. We don't know for certain as parents or caregivers if the person we're caring for really understands what we're saying. So we have the tendency to hammer home certain basics to increase the chance of the information getting through. Sometimes we're subtle in our approach and other times we find the need to be more direct with the information.

Just as we do with our children or family members or society member we care for – our Spirit provides us with much guidance along the way. Sometimes our Spirits leave subtle hints and gifts of information and other times they help us create situations that bring us information more directly. Our Spirits have an excellent idea of what information we're getting and what we are not. Our Spirits also make no judgments on the lessons we learn, on the information we process, and the information we don't process. They simply take joy in being a participant.

We can learn from our Spirits and detach a bit from whether or not our kin fully integrate what we hammer home. We trust the angels and Spirit will watch over them. This gives us the opportunity to take a bit more joy in being part of the process. We can focus more on the things they are getting; or we can reassess what to subtly express and what to hammer home more efficiently. As we move forward with love and compassion for ourselves and those around us, we choose to see the Light in each person shine. Perhaps we'll choose to gently hammer home the greatness of their Light. In doing so, our self-perception as well as our perception of others, shifts towards inspiration and possibilities.

Week 2 Reflection Exercise

Think of something someone has in the past or is currently now, hammering home to you – whether it is job related, school related, or family/self related.

Are you getting the message or are you resisting the message? If you are resisting the message, see if you can determine why. Is it because it wasn't your idea? Or because of who is telling it to you?

Think of some thought or aspect that you are attempting to hammer home with someone in your life.

Are they getting the message or are they resisting it?

Are there other ways you can get your point across without being pushy? Is it time to back off a little while so they can integrate your perspective?

This week, make it a point to compliment the people you care for and those who care for you.

Week 2 Affirmation

I trust myself to share applicable life lessons with others. I allow others time and space to integrate and accept those life lessons as they choose.

Week 3
Holding the Flame

We can look at holding the flame as a game we play
with ourselves. Each of us holds a flame in our hearts.
Some days it shines brightly; other days, it shines a
bit more dimly. Our responsibility is to hold that
flame as brightly as possible in any situation while being careful not to judge or compare our present flame
to other moments or other people's flames. We simply
hold our flame as brightly as we can at that given moment.

The challenge arises when we feel agitated, stuck, angry, or trapped. The challenge can remain when we
feel as though we want to walk away from everyone
and everything and be in a different place; when we're
playing the victim and not knowing how to get out of
it; when we're tired of working hard and possibly feeling owed a different life.

Holding the flame means persistently trusting in the
light within us even when our spirits seem tired – when
we seem tired of trying, tired of reaching for glim-
mers of light that seem so far away; tired of people
telling us we're not good enough; tired of not accepting ourselves for who we are; tired of feeling expec-

tations from others; tired of trying to be there for everyone and being supportive all the time, yet feeling that so little is returned.

Holding the flame is finding that change of heart, allowing the change of heart to occur, letting us know we still hold the flame inside. It can be something we do, or something we witness, or something someone says to us that inspires that change of heart. It's remaining open enough to allow our hearts to shift and our minds to focus thoughts on uplifting topics. Holding the flame is making sure that we can always find that spark, even in the darker moments; allowing experiences to unfold that help us along when we seem to lack the energy or realization to do so.

Holding the flame is always making sure we can find the flame of light in our hearts, regardless of what's going on outside and inside of us. It's allowing the internal struggle and understanding that the struggle may be part of the journey. It's seeing and feeling that light inside of us regardless how small - even during the short periods of time we find we might not like ourselves. It's knowing that we can shine, all the time, if we make the decision to do so.

Week 3 Reflection Exercise

Think of something that makes you smile every time you think about it. Focus on this experience, place, object, etc., for a few moments, so your smile fills your entire being.

Now bring to mind a moment where you felt sad, miserable, or depressed. During that situation, try to recall if there were any external factors during that moment that went unnoticed – was someone trying to distract you, did a pet nudge you for attention, did the sun temporarily break through the clouds, did a much loved song come on the radio, etc?

Do you remember allowing any good thoughts to enter your mind?

What would have happened to your experience if you allowed the thing that makes you smile every time enter your consciousness?

This week, if there are moments when your inner light seems dim, try to be more aware of the small potentially uplifting details around you. Or tug upon your own happy moments to help ease yourself out of the dim moment into a brighter one.

Week 3 Affirmation

I am open and willing to see and receive Joy at all times.

Week 4
Besting a Moment

Besting a moment is finding a jewel in the ordinary or dreaded moment. To find the jewel, we must take time to evaluate ourselves in the situation. Does the situation force us to face a fear? Does it give us an opportunity to express who we are with compassion and love? Does the situation bring with it the potential for others to reject us? Does it give us a chance to determine what we will choose to be affected by?

Once we understand our fear a bit better we can start shaping thoughts to help remove that fear or work our way into acceptance of the situation. Sometimes the ability to move through the fear and into acceptance is the jewel itself. Normally, once we pass through fear and accept a situation for what it is, we've freed our mind enough to see the situation with a new, fresh perspective. How the situation is resolved or carried out changes drastically based on this new perspective. Sometimes our new outlook affects others in the situation, changing the dynamic yet again. Everyone in the situation has the opportunity to grow by us taking the first step in besting a moment.

Week 4 Reflection Exercise

Think of a task or situation that you seem to be dreading.

See if you can determine what the primary, base source of the dread is.

Ask yourself how you can best face this situation. What potential jewel (no matter how small) in the experience is hidden there?

Take a few moments to visualize you experiencing the task or situation in the best possible way. Provide as much detail with the intent and emotion behind the experience. Allow this visualization to hold the highest good for all involved. Surround this visualization in brilliant pink light or energy – a Love vibration. Let go of any attachment to the outcome and see what happens.

Week 4 Affirmation

I am open to transforming my fears into opportunities to learn and grow.

Week 5
Seizing a Moment

Seizing a moment is realizing in one moment all the potential positives for that moment previously not realized. It's realizing that we can do, or say something that would change the moment from feeling ok to feeling wonderful. There is no dread or preparation experienced before this moment. It is a pure moment, and one that reflects our openness to creating our experiences. Some folks seize a moment invoking laughter into an otherwise tense or serious conversation. Other folks boost the confidence of their peers or simply share who they are.

There are plenty of opportunities for us to seize a moment for our own personal fun, laughter, progress, and self esteem. We can also experiment with being aware of seizing a moment to make someone else's moment more grand. It is about allowing us that benefit of being in the moment – fully and emotionally in the moment - participating, and capturing the minute aspects of that moment rather than looking feverishly into the future for the next one.

As we build on our seizing moments throughout the day, we'll have applied enough energy to seize the day.

Week 5 Reflection Exercise

Think of a time where you feel you seized an opportunity, right then in the moment, with no previous consideration.

Consider some moments where you allowed opportunities to pass by – where you thought of seizing the moment but didn't.

What is the difference in the feeling of each scenario?

This week, seize at least five moments for laughter or heartfelt experiences – for yourself and for others.

Week 5 Affirmation

I openly and easily flow into expressing moments of love and laughter throughout my days.

Week 6
Cultivating a Moment

There is a moment when we walk into a planned event and we know, we feel, we appreciate the work and inspiration that went into creating that event. Weddings or other types of gatherings are perfect examples of when people may take time to witness and appreciate all the planning and thought that went into creating the event. We learn to tell when the moment has been carefully cultivated, and when it has not.

Cultivating a moment certainly may not require a lot of time, money or practice. All it really takes is quality in focus. It entails knowing what you want, knowing how you want the moment to feel and how you may wish others to feel as well. Although we cannot be solely responsible for other people's reactions – for their openness and judgment on the moment is truly subjective - we can set a certain ambience, or plan a series of moments.

When creating moments for ourselves, we may not always know what we want. It's great to explore our options and learn more about how we want to live our moments. We can create fun moments for ourselves; we can cultivate the characteristics we value in our moments and if we wish, find others to share them with. Each moment we cultivate for ourselves or for others, brings us the opportunity to grow and nurture ourselves into being the best person we can be within each moment.

Week 6 Reflection Exercise

Think of a moment or event that you attended or created and thought or commented that this was a really well thought out and planned event – a moment that was definitely cultivated.

Think back of a time when you cultivated and worked towards a specific moment. How did it feel? Was it all you had dreamed or did you learn there were some things that could have gone differently?

Is there a moment or event that you've been wanting to cultivate but haven't?

If so, this week, take a few steps to start cultivating this moment. If not, take some time this week to identify some moments that you would like to cultivate and brainstorm ideas on how to do so.

Week 6 Affirmation

I am capable of openly cultivating loving, safe, fun moments for me and others.

Week 7
Take it in Stride

Taking things in stride is seemingly much easier said than done, especially when things seem to be going in the opposite direction of the way we planned. Yet, we all know or have known people who seem to do this so well - that nothing really aggravates them, they simply pause, or not, and redirect their thoughts to address the new situation. It's really quite amazing and admirable to see this in action. For some of us, we may find it easier to have this ability occur in certain areas of our lives, but not yet across the board.

The main issue that seems to keep us from taking things in stride is an attachment to a specific outcome. Another cause may be feeling as though we're losing control. When something goes awry during our workday or family gathering, we may immediately become depressed or angry. Whether we've attached importance to that end result personally, or collectively, results in some discordant emotion arising. Once we have an attachment to a specific result that does not occur we may wind up taking our thoughts into a downward spiral.

However, the evaluation of the situation can be viewed without judgment, which enables us to easily move from one end result to another. Better planning and setting expectations may help as well. Regardless, we can certainly learn from the experiences and how we'd like to do them differently if a next time occurs.

As we grow spiritually, we must learn to lose our attachment to a given outcome. We can stop giving our personal power over to a specific situation. Allowing a situation to make or break our day discounts our value as individuals and keeps us stuck in a particular mindset. It's clearly our judgment of a situation that allows it to affect our day. When we choose to let go of the judgment, we open up an ability to take things in stride.

Let's challenge ourselves to be less judgmental with daily situations and take each item in stride as best as possible. Learn to understand our own reactions that reflect our attachments to specific situations. As we let go of those attachments, we find our ability to take things in stride improves.

Week 7 Reflection Exercise

Consider a recent occurrence where you felt yourself resisting the way a situation was playing out. How did you react? Why did you react that way?

How could you have responded to the point you were taking the situation in stride, while still maintaining your integrity and honesty?

This week see if you can take something in stride a bit more easily than you normally do. Be aware of when others are taking things in stride better than you'd expected, or more than you would have were you to be in their shoes.

Week 7 Affirmation

I easily go with the flow of life. I adapt easily and quickly to what life brings my way.

Week 8
Loving the Process

As with all processes we follow – whether it be drying dishes or putting away laundry, or building a fire – there are various steps within a process that we enjoy more than other steps within the same process. We may rush through the less pleasant steps and prolong the more favored steps. This is a natural thing to do.

With just the right perspective, we can learn to appreciate and savor each step along the process without judgment. When we find a place in our path that we're not as "happy" about, we can take the time to find out why. What sort of insecurities is it bringing up for us? What about that specific step can we learn to appreciate? Can we become better at this step or is it time to change the process to more efficient steps that may combine or eliminate some of the not so pleasant steps? Is there a level of acceptance we must have for a specific step that we seem to resist?

Any time a discordant emotion arises is a perfect time for us to sit back and determine why. We can even spend a few minutes evaluating why we enjoy a step as well; giving us time to savor it and appreciate it even more.

The more we take the time to be aware of what we enjoy and what we can learn, the easier we can tell where things are for us. Our resistance becomes less intense, and we're able to adapt or change where we need to, allowing for a less stressful situation or life.

Although we may allow our focus to be the end result of a process, it's more often the process of getting there that is the real prize.

Week 8 Reflection Exercise:

Take a moment and make a list of some tasks that you typically rush through with little regard to the actual task itself. These tasks would be ones where the focus is on completing the task quickly so you may move to something perceived as more fun or meaningful.

Choose one of the tasks on the list. Write down some ideas on how to enjoy the process itself – why do you usually rush through it?

The next time you perform that task, slow yourself down and attempt to be very consciously aware of each action you make or each word you choose.

As the week progresses, see if you can find yourself approaching these tasks with mindfulness of the task itself – where great attention to how each step of the task is accomplished. Record or talk with someone about how it felt different than rushing through it.

Week 8 Affirmation

I find joy and acceptance in the tasks I perform each day.

Week 9
Expression of Self

We all choose how we wish to express ourselves – there is great variety in how we do so. Some of us change our appearance, speech, values, and beliefs - all to express ourselves as who we are at that moment.

There are also many of us who do not express ourselves, or only express ourselves behind closed doors, in private, in situations where we feel more safe. Yet, at the core of human expression, we long to express ourselves all the time, in all situations, even when we have learned that it is not appropriate to do so in certain situations. Again, at the core of human expression, there is no judgment on what is expressed – only joy in the expression and ability of one to express themselves.

When we become comfortable with who we are, where we want to be, and the steps we're taking to get there, it becomes easier to express ourselves. Once we have accepted ourselves and the way in which we feel we wish to express ourselves, we find no need to justify our actions or thoughts. We find no need to wish others understood us. We find no need to push our thoughts and beliefs on others. We reach a point where we are a-okay with who we are and a-okay if others aren't a-okay with us. We learn to go with the flow and keep focus on what our self-expression entails without infringing upon someone else's and move on.

Self-expression at the core is true harmony - harmony with all there is inside of us, and then harmony with all there is outside of us. We are walking masters of the universe, in our true state of self-expression. We are LOVE.

Week 9 Reflection Exercise

Think of a moment where you suppressed your ability to express yourself? How did it feel?

Is there a way in which you could have expressed yourself with love and compassion?

Think of a moment where you expressed yourself freely? How did that feel?

Did you express yourself with love and compassion, without infringing upon someone else's self expression?

This week, take some time to find ways (no matter how small) to express yourself with love and compassion in areas where you might have suppressed your expression. In kind, celebrate the moments where you did express yourself as well.

Week 9 Affirmation

I easily discern and enact appropriate ways to express my being.

Making a Mess

We've all made messes in our lifetimes – we've had the opportunity to make physical messes, emotional messes, relationship messes, and even artistic ones.

Some messes we enjoy making and others we don't even know we were making them until we find our-selves standing in the middle of it – literally or figura-tively. Some of us really dislike messes – especially when we're the ones who need to clean it up. Keep in mind, there are times when making a mess is quite ne-cessary – like that of a messy diaper, or a messy kitchen after a home cooked meal, or a messy room full of half empty boxes after a move or in prepara-tion of a move. We seem to get so caught up in the work needed in cleaning the mess we don't take time to analyze or appreciate the mess.

What if we were to take time viewing the mess and feeling what went behind that mess – determining the potential reasons for the mess? Was the mess created through fun and laughter; was it bred with creativity and passion; was it a necessary release? Or is the mess an end result of greed, laziness manipula-tion or selfishness?

In all we do, we have the opportunity to make a mess. Messes may certainly be a part of our lives. Sometimes we need to create some sort of disruption of order to maintain an appreciation of that order. Similar to a spool of thread - we can unravel a spool of thread - and we can ravel it back up if we want or we can cut what we've unraveled and use it. We must learn to do the same with our perceived messes - do we ravel them back up and periodically unravel it again, or do we make use of the mess that's laid out in front of us and weave it into something beautiful?

Week 10 Reflection Exercise

Consider a time where you came across a mess – literally or figuratively in your life – a relationship mess, a messy room or kitchen, etc. Were you discouraged? Angry? Or did it bring laughter to you?

Do you understand now or did you then, understand what went behind the mess – the reasons for it?

Next time you're confronted with a mess, take a few moments to consider all that went behind creating that mess. Then determine if you would like to prevent a mess like this from happening again or if you would like to support its evolution.

If you would like to support the mess's evolution or contain it more, how can you better do so in the future?

Week 10 Affirmation

I understand that messes occur and take the time to understand their existence as it pertains to me.

Week 11
Cleaning Up

Cleaning up is often perceived as a chore most people try to avoid or complete quickly. A messy office, dirty dishes or laundry, or relationships gone awry usually send people looking for other things to do than face the clean up. And understandably so - cleaning up messes can be dirty, awk- ward and in some cases, full of guilt and shame.

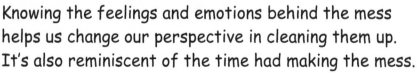

But beyond these aspects, often, cleaning up the mess is where we find some of greatest gifts. We may learn a new skill. We may learn something about our- selves or about someone else that we hadn't realized before. We learn about life. In cleaning up the mess, we can sometimes relive mo- ments of creating the mess. Knowing the feelings and emotions behind the mess helps us change our perspective in cleaning them up. It's also reminiscent of the time had making the mess.

Whether it is a party, or a painting, cleaning up gives us a chance to savor the time just spent, or builds determination to do things differently next time. Cleaning up also allows us the space to accept fully where we are, perhaps with a glimpse of where we wish to be. Cleaning up may signify that we took a challenge or a step forward in doing something or we reacted to a situation with the best we had at that moment. The situation may have worked well, it may not have. Cleaning up gives us tools we can use in preventing future messes or cleaning them up.

Week 11 Reflection Exercise

Think of a recent mess you had to clean up. Were you upset, indifferent, or happy to clean up the mess? And why? Usually the reason the mess was made helps in our demeanor of cleaning up.

Did you rush through the clean up or did you find yourself reminiscing about making the mess while cleaning up?

This week, allow yourself to fully understand the reasons for a situation to have occurred. Reflect upon what you learned, appreciated, obtained by taking the steps to clean it up.

Week 11 Affirmation

I am open to learning from the perceived messes in my life.

Week 12
Walking your Path

There comes a point in time where we've explored our options, explored our interests, and we've determined where we believe we want to go. We know what we want to do – how we want to live our lives; yet, there may seem to be some reason not to. It may be an attachment to who we are or not letting go of our own and others' perceptions of who we are that holds us back from doing what we desire to do. Fearful thoughts arise...*if we change what will happen to this relationship?*

Fear of where change may take us is normal. If we take time to experience the fear, get to know it, become familiar with it, the reason for being afraid no longer frightens us. We take steps to minimize our fear and move forward.

Walking our Path is walking our Truth. It's knowing where our truth ends and where someone else's begins. It's trusting ourselves enough to know when to speak and when to be silent. It's respecting our own truth and respecting everyone else's. It's sharing our truth with love and compassion without any attachment to what the outcome is - simply sharing to share and be in joy in sharing.

Walking our Path is taking steps to being who we truly are – not what others believe or expect us to be. Once we have made a decision, then we alone are accountable for making progress. The choice is ours. We can choose to love our path, appreciate our path; walk it with confidence and in joy. We can choose to walk with pride and grace, enjoying and observing those whose paths cross ours and take in the scenery along the way.

Week 12 Reflection Exercise

List out some major or minor decisions you've made that caused change in your life.

Select one in particular where people did not support your change or another decision that you made that you were afraid of. What thoughts arise surrounding this decision? Do you know why you were afraid or why others did not support you/the decision?

Did the decision make you trust yourself or distrust yourself? What have you learned from making the decision? What have you learned about trusting others or questioning their support?

What have you learned about trusting and supporting yourself?

Take a moment to acknowledge that you walked your path in this decision making process.

Consider a decision in the future that helps define the path you're walking.

Week 12 Affirmation
I respect myself enough to walk my own path and allow
others to walk theirs without judgment.

Week 13
Drumbeat

The drumbeat reminds us and teaches us to notice
rhythms all around us – the rhythm of the days,
weeks, moon, sea, and the seasons. We are deeply con-
nected to our drumbeat, the rhythm of our Soul. It
leads us to where we need to be if we're open to its
harkening. The drumbeat of our Soul soothes us and
gently guides us to our hearts' desires.

When we take the time to close our eyes and settle
our minds, and we allow the emotions to pass through
our bodies, we find ourselves in a place where no-thing
exists. In this space we can be, see, and feel who we
truly are. We can take note of the pace of our growth,
the rhythm of our natural progressions, our ebbs and
flows. This is our drumbeat. This is the beat that our
souls are creating together with each of us individually, and in harmony with one another.

We can choose to go within and connect with the flow
with this rhythm, to where we become instinctively
inspired to reach our highest potential, in this human
form.

Week 13 Reflection Exercise

Take a few moments to feel and listen to the rhythm of your breath. Is the breath long or short?

Allow the breath to change its rhythm on its own. Simply through awareness the breath will begin to change and find another rhythm – still yours, but more aware.

Sit for 3-5 minutes simply being aware of and focusing only on your breath.

This week, find moments to be aware of the rhythm of your breath. Sit with it for as short or as long as you like. Dare to lose yourself in the rhythm of your breath.

Week 13 Affirmation

I am in tune with the rhythm of my life.

Week 14
Chocolate Covered Cherry (Triple C)

For some of us, chocolate covered cherries are a rare treat. A chocolate covered cherry is easily selected from an assortment of chocolates. It's one with the rounded top, just the right "cherry covered" size, and it has a flat cylindrical base. It beckons us to try it.

When we bite a triple C for the first time, the sweet liquid surrounding the cherry may drip down our chin and into our hands. We learn quickly that there is a certain way to handle the triple C when we eat it. Although it is quite firm on the outside, the inside is soft and partially full of thick liquid.

The way we bite into the triple C is much different than we would bite into an apple. We know we only need to get past the first layer of chocolate and ease up once we've passed that point.

How we approach different life situations is similar. There are times when we know we have a triple C situation on our hands – a seemingly tough, delicate circumstance. Yet we still sink our teeth into it as if it is a crisp granny smith apple or gnaw on it as if it is a piece of beef jerky. Without thoroughly feeling and discerning how to handle the people or situation, we find things in a general state of disarray.

Or there may be times we are frightened by the situation and don't sink our teeth in with enough fervor to make a difference. We may have sensitive teeth and are afraid to bite down on the hard outer layer for fear of pain, or fear the sweetness inside may cause some discomfort as well.

With triple C situations, we realize there are levels that we need to be aware of. From this awareness we can discern our points of participation in those levels. Knowing or feeling how long to stay at each level, is also helpful. With awareness during a triple C real life execution, we can find the best Chocolate Covered Cherry, and its decadent sweetness, in the midst of a seemingly stress-ridden day.

Week 14 Reflection Exercise

Think of a time where you entered a situation with great gusto when it really needed a softer approach. How did that feel? When did you realize that the softer approach was needed?

What emotions surrounded your intention and thought to move into the situation with gusto?

Were you able to decrease the intensity of your involvement successfully for all those involved?

What are you able to glean from the situation that helps you be more aware of the necessary approach for future experiences?

This week, be aware of your involvement in specific situations. Determine if your approach is appropriate for what you wish to gain from it, and from the perspective of others.

Week 14 Affirmation

I use an accurate balance of sensitivity and strength throughout my days.

Week 15

Stay Awake

We all have moments of inspiration, elation and experiences of a higher vibration. In most cases, we know how to attain this elation, we know the focus it takes, and we understand the openness it requires. More often than not, we long to be in that state consistently. Some of us believe, though, that once we've attained that state that it cannot be held for long periods of time; that through interaction with others and involvement in activities other than the inspiring activity, we cannot maintain the elation.

While each day our best and our experiences vary, we are consistently raising our own vibration and that of those around us. It doesn't always feel like we are, and that may be because we allow ourselves to get sucked back into the realm of worry, judgment, fear, and disassociated emotions. We need to make the commitment of being strong inside before we can approach the world outside of us with that same strength. Our awareness of what is and what is not, our clarity of viewing situations from beneath the surface rather than on the surface, provides us more confidence in our own abilities and our actions or non-actions to situations in our lives. Without keeping that higher perspective and staying awake at the wheel, we increase the risk of falling back into the abyss of drama and emotionality.

Through consistent emotional, mental, physical, and spiritual awareness, we are able to withstand the heartiest of items perceived as not good in this world; knowing, or at least learning to decipher their true deeper meaning to us and others involved.

Staying awake in life is attainable. It requires focus, commitment, and time. With consistent practice and diligence, our lives will unfold with joy and love more often, changing our world, thus changing THE world.

Week 15 Reflection Exercise
Staying Awake is, in essence, what this book is helping us become – more aware of items below the surface – digging deeper into ourselves, analyzing our emotional, mental, and spiritual involvement in life situations.

This week, select an exercise from a previous chapter in this book and work with it this week again. You may choose one you had specific difficulty or one that you flowed with in ease. The choice is yours.

Week 15 Affirmation
I enjoy being aware.

Week 16
Confirmation of Self

Once we've decided who it is we want to be, we find
there are things about us we'd like to change – there
are different aspects about ourselves, characteristics, habits, thought processes, etc., that we would
like to alter. There may be times when making those
changes may seem daunting and difficult, but all we
really need to do is make that choice. We may not act
the way we would like to all of the time, but our
awareness of our actions during and after a situation
enable us to understand more fully our own interactions and ways to alter to them.

Confirmation of self also requires permission from
ourselves to be who we want to be. Even though we
may have made the decision to be our own person,
there are limiting patterns of behavior and thinking
that we are tied to - expectations and past experiences - that keep us from giving ourselves complete
permission to be who we really wish to be, who we really are.

During our path we must take the time to realize how
far we have come – to note all our little wins. If we
focus on the positive thoughts and actions we have

and take throughout each day we won't have time or even notice any potential items we could beat ourselves up about.

Others may even point out some positives to us, dropping little hints to help guide us along the way. Only we know the true challenges and the true victories of our paths. Only we know when we're being true to ourselves. By choosing to confirm our progress and ourselves each step of the way, moment by moment, we find ourselves enjoying our choices fully and openly.

Week 16 Reflection Exercise

Spend a few moments thinking about aspects you wanted to change about yourself within the past year. These aspects could be in the form of wanting to be more patient, less reactive, more trusting, less judgmental, etc.

Select three of the aspects. Have you successfully changed these aspects? Do you see progress being made? Can you define a moment where you mentally noted that you can make a change? Or can you define a moment where you did make a change? How did it feel?

Regardless how small or large you perceive the progress to be, take note of the progress and acknowledge it. If you so feel inclined, perform a mini celebration in honor of your progress.

Week 16 Affirmation

I consistently take active steps in reaching my goals of personal improvement.

Week 17
The World in a Moment

Envision bubbles all around. Within each bubble imagine a special world that exists – a living world in each bubble.

Now...imagine each bubble is a moment. Each bubble, each moment, is moving, existing, changing all the time. As we look around, we are surrounded by myriads of bubbles and moments. When we focus on just one bubble - one moment - all the rest of the moments and bubbles move to the background of our consciousness, so we're focusing only on that one bubble.

As we watch each moment, we notice that each one contains a treasure box. The treasure boxes may be difficult to find in some moments, yet if we look long enough, we find the treasure and admire its beauty. We leave the treasure there for others to find then move on to our next moment. In some cases, the treasure boxes may be empty, giving us the opportunity to place a treasure inside if we choose to do so. We may even take a small piece of treasure from one bubble to another bubble.

We hold the world in our hands each moment. Our world changes when we live and view each moment with open treasure boxes. Within each moment exists a spark. We can choose to ignite that spark, or let it fall to the wayside. We can play the spectator and watch our bubbles float by or immerse ourselves in each moment bubble to experience the Light inside.

We can take note of the treasure boxes in each moment throughout our days. We can notice which ones need a treasure placed in it and which ones already have one. With continued attention on our moments, we're able to understand our world each moment at a time and treasure each one.

Week 17 Reflection Exercise

We all have experienced matters where we judge a specific experience as meaningless. Consider a time recently where you felt that what you did at that moment would make no difference to you or anyone else.

Next time you feel this way, take a step back and attempt to perceive the situation as its own world – regardless how small or large you deem it to be.

Act as if the moment is being watched by the world – and affected by all. Know that your vibration and intention are rippled through the furniture, space, people, plants, environment that you coexist with. All your thoughts and actions ripple out to the world and return to you at some later date.

Choose how you react to or move through a seeming unimportant task to be one of great importance.

Week 17 Affirmation

Each of my thoughts and actions are reflections how I view my world.

Week 18
Following the Lure

Following a lure may be perceived as a not so good thing. The word lure itself offers a tone of trickiness to it. Yet the phrase "following the lure" indicates some amount of innocence, desire, and openness. To follow a lure, you first have to know and be aware that it exists. Then we must discern on whether to follow it.

Many of us ignore the lures of our hearts' desires. We may come across some items that seem too good to be true or even deceiving at first glance. Using our own discernment, we then determine if the lure is something to follow. Keep in mind just because we've decided to follow a lure, doesn't necessarily mean we're going to sink our teeth into it. Following the lure means we're following it to see where it takes us, exploring our options. Sometimes, the exploration is learning and education enough.

If we're following our hearts, we can only be brought into spaces of Light. We get to find out if the lure is a stepping-stone to something else or the beginning of a life long journey. We'll only know if we take a chance, discern for ourselves, and follow that tugging of our hearts, and lure our lives into Joy.

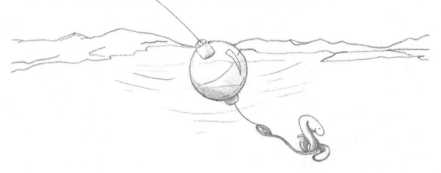

Week 18 Reflection Exercise

Consider a moment where you wanted to do something heartfelt and for some reason or another you stopped yourself from doing so. How did it feel?

Now consider a time where you started or completely followed through on a heartfelt action or desire. How did it feel then?

This week, take a moment every day to list out moments where you've stopped yourself from following your heart as well as the moments you let yourself follow a heartfelt desire. For those times you didn't, try to answer why.

For those times you did, revel in the joy the experiences provided you.

Week 18 Affirmation

I revel in the joy and experiences of my life.

Week 19
Facing the Hook

When we've followed the lure enough to our satisfaction, there comes a time to determine if we're going to commit further or not. This crucial decision can be made with ease, or we can labor over the choice. Facing the hook is where we're deciding whether to fully commit to the bait.

Many of us choose to stand in this spot for some time – hoping some circumstance will help make the decision by pushing us one way, or omitting an option - or that something else will come along that keeps us preoccupied and distracted from making a decision.

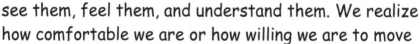

Sometimes, though, the decision is exactly what we've asked for or what we've wanted. Yet we have sincere reservations about making the step. As the fears surface, we give ourselves a chance to really see them, feel them, and understand them. We realize how comfortable we are or how willing we are to move forward with the item in question. We take into consideration the ramifications of the potential steps forward – the responsibilities we must hold, the people who may be affected. Then again, we may not. We may know instinctively that this is what we're looking for, without any logical explanation.

This is all part of self-discovery. Regardless what happens from this point forward, bringing to the surface all the emotions, doubts, fears, excitement, and joy that accompany facing the hook, provides growth for us. We have the opportunity to release fears, to step into excitement – to understand what the proposed endeavor or change feels like.

 If the choice is made to walk away, so be it. If the choice is made to move forward, so be it. Each choice is part of our path.

Week 19 Reflection Exercise

Think of a time where you were faced with doing something you always wanted to do.

Did you follow through? Did you feel ready? Did you have enough information?

What doubts or fears arose? What exciting, anticipatory emotions came to the surface?

What did you learn?

How will you allow that experience help you make future decisions?

Week 19 Affirmation

I trust myself to make accurate decisions.

Week 20
Taking the Bait

Our decision has been made. We've followed the lure
long or short enough to know we want to commit a bit
more. We take the bait. We allow ourselves to let go
of controlling the outcome; we allow ourselves to trust
in the situation and let go or surrender all the fears
or justifications that arose. We've taken a major step
forward.

Taking the bait does include some amount of surrender. We acknowledge that this is new ground for us.
We acknowledge that part of it may scare us. We
know that part of it excites us. And here we are, on
our way – totally open, totally free, moving forward
with openness and awareness.

This line could be short and sweet – the experiences
joyous and light. Or the bait could bring us experiences that raise more issues to the foreground.
Whatever the case, it's all good; it's all divine. We
commend ourselves for walking this path.

Week 20 Reflection Exercise

What experiences in your life are you currently testing the waters on? This could be a new job, different relationship, new look, different class or project, etc.

Are you enjoying the ride so far?

Are you open to what the experience has to offer you?

Are you ready to let go of the experience and move on or hold on to it and take it one step further?

This week, see if there are any situations you need to let go of or move into more fully.

Week 20 Affirmation

I easily recognize the need to flow in and out of experiences for my highest good.

Week 21

Being Caught

Once we've done our research and feel comfortable with where we're going, once we've bitten the bait and committed to the ride, we start to see things differently than ever before, if we allow ourselves to.

Sometimes we resist because the line is being drawn in too quickly. Other times, we clamp down and enjoy the ride – the water flashing on either side of us, moving us through a situation with ease and speed. Once the situation takes us out of the waters, we may experience gripping fear. Or we may stand in awe and wonder taking everything in.

When we follow the direction of hearts, it may involve letting go of something so another something even better may enter into our lives. More often than not, Spirit tosses us either back in the waters we came from, so we have a chance to view those waters with a change in perception or into completely new waters where we learn to adapt and adjust as is best for our growth. Because we have allowed ourselves the experience of being caught in the situation, or drawn to a certain experience, we can now view our world differently – swim a bit differently, socialize a bit differently, simply exist a bit differently.

Sometimes the process may make us feel as though we're exhausted and overwhelmed with emotions of fear and sadness. Other times we hit the water again feeling exhilarated, and joyous. Either way, we return to the waters or face our next step with courage, determination, and a different viewpoint. The differences may be subtle or not so subtle to those around us. What matters is that we are aware of them.

Our world changes each time we follow that lure from Spirit. We know when to hang on for the ride, and when to release our bite when we've had enough. We go with the flow. We allow ourselves to be caught up in a moment, caught off guard by the beauty or fear of an experience, view the world through the eyes of our innocent ones, and begin to experience the beings we truly are.

Week 21 Reflection Exercise

Think of a moment that seems to have changed your life. How did this experience change your perception of yourself?

How did this experience change your perception of others?

What knowledge or skill did you learn from the experience?

This week, take note of the skills and knowledge you have. Think back to the experiences in your life that provided you that skill or knowledge. Thank yourself for adapting and acquiring new aspects and bringing them with you to help enhance your life and the lives of those around you. Each moment is a chance to learn and grow.

Week 21 Affirmation

I am open to learning from life's experiences.

Love Unconditionally

Loving unconditionally is a choice. Judging someone and speaking harshly to someone is a choice. Treating someone with compassion and patience is also a choice. They may be learned reactions, but still a choice to allow that learned reaction to be experienced.

In order to love others unconditionally, we must learn to love ourselves as such. Many of us know this intellectually already, yet living it in our hearts is the next step. We must learn to love ourselves unconditionally before we can learn to love others unconditionally. Unconditionally is a robust word. It seems a lot to ask.

Throughout our journey, our outer world will reflect our inner world. Our conflicts in our outer world denote our inner self-conflicts – items we have not yet resolved or come to peace with. The more lovingly we allow ourselves to resolve our internal conflicts, the more easily it is to love others as they go through their own internal conflicts and process.

When we are confronted with a person who feels angry, sad, or inadequate, we can make it a point to put ourselves in that person's shoes. We may also find some of the same aspects within ourselves that make us feel angry, sad or inadequate. We can attempt to understand with compassion and grace, what they are experiencing, and reflect on a time when we had similar feelings. We can consider how we would feel if someone lovingly responded rather than harshly reacted. In following this process throughout the day, we can become more loving towards others and ourselves simultaneously.

Week 22 Reflection Exercise

Think about today and your mental conversations with yourself. How many of the conversations were loving and compassionate? How many were filled with ridicule, criticism, and self doubt?

What emotions arose at the time of the mental conversations? How did you feel about yourself?

Now think about the conversations you had with others today. How many of the conversations were loving and compassionate? How many were filled with ridicule, criticism, or blame?

This week, monitor your thoughts and words to yourself. If you like, you may keep a tally of the times you are loving and compassionate with yourself versus the times you were critical. Attempt to change your words on the spot – see how your self image changes.

Once you feel comfortable doing this with yourself, carry the awareness to your conversations with others.

Week 22 Affirmation

I extend and accept unconditional love.

Week 23
Filling My Cup

Many of us go about our days ensuring that everyone else is taken care of; our family members, our friends, our coworkers' expectations and needs are sometimes met before or while addressing our own. We live in a world of multitasking, multi-media, and multiplexes. The more we can accomplish at once, the better.

In living at a hurried pace, we find our energy levels depleted and our mental and physical bodies working overtime. Even if we're not living this pace, we are still participating in our work and dealing with family and friends who usually are living at that pace. To be our best during our work and leisure activities, it's essential for our own mental, physical, and emotional well being to be addressed before assisting or working with others. It takes practice and discipline to find what works for us as well as time. We need to allow ourselves the time to achieve the desired result and determine the suitable method for us to replenish ourselves.

To have a calm and open outlook on situations, centering our own beings becomes important to us. We find rituals or meditations or some focus that enables us to fill ourselves with the energy we need to face the day or situation. We realize that filling our cups with whatever we feel we need means being able to give more to others and ourselves without running low.

Week 23 Reflection Exercise

In the midst of a stressful day, do you take the time to periodically center yourself? If so, how do you do this?

Do you know when you need to breathe more deeply or step outdoors? Have you ever done so as a preventative measure as opposed to a corrective or necessary measure?

Write a list of activities or non-activities that you find help you relax – exercise, being outdoors, meditating, gardening, watching a movie, etc.

This week, tally up the number of times you find yourself partaking in items from that list. Determine if this number seems appropriate or if it can be increased with positive results. You may also choose to note what, if anything, is holding you back from nurturing yourself with your relaxing items.

Week 23 Affirmation

I take time to nurture my being.

Week 24

Curing the Cough

Coughs may be caused or brought on by various factors including too much physical activity, infection,
cold, etc. Regardless of the cause, a cough signifies an
interruption in the flow of air. We may drink a glass
of water to cure the dry cough; we take over the
counter cold medicines or other remedies to help
clear our passageway. There are even some days our
cough is so bad that we take time away from our normal activities to rest while the passageways clear. We
do what it takes so our breathing returns to normal or
to optimal levels so we may function throughout our
days.

In life, there may be many things that cause pauses or
unexpected breaks in the flow – little hiccups or
coughs where we find ourselves stopping to take time
to appropriately deal with whatever is contributing to
the interruption in flow. It could be an unexpected
comment that someone says, previously bottled up
emotions that may have surfaced, or just a complete
lack of feeling in general.

Whatever causes us to breathe less optimally, rest
assured, there's always a cure, and we get past it. We

address what we need to – we clear that which blocks us from breathing easily, we face the fears we need to - and continue to move forward. Some coughs take a little longer to cure than others, and some coughs even come back periodically and that's ok. We're making it through the best we can, taking personal inventory through awareness and perhaps meditation to know when to push ourselves a little more, or to rest a little more.

We are here on earth to learn about ourselves – to learn about humanity - individually and as a whole. We all experience individual and collective coughs at times. By making a concerted effort and setting aside time to determine what is causing the cough, we can learn appropriately how to remove the cause and clear our passageway to clarity.

Week 24 Reflection Exercise

List any hiccups you may be experiencing in your life now. Are there issues with a current relationship or aspect of your life that up until now has been going smoothly?

If you have not yet, take a few moments to determine why you think these hiccups are occurring. Have you been avoiding addressing them? Have you been putting too much energy towards them? Are you allowing yourself or them to breathe?

Are there any specific formulas to the situation that you know make things smooth sailing?

This week, when you feel something blocking the flow of a situation, take a step back and see what solutions you can offer from your heart.

Week 24 Affirmation

I take time to address emotions that are blocking my life's flow.

Week 25

Joy in the World

Seeing or finding joy in the world is a matter of perspective. Certain things or situations going on in our
lives may diminish our mood and our ability to be
joyous. Some of us compartmentalize our joy and only
retrieve that emotion at specific times. We lift the
lid and choose a specific or perceived appropriate expression of joy rather than letting the joy express
itself fluidly. Many times we speed through our days
with such focus and activity that we prevent ourselves
from ever seeing or being aware of opportunities to
be joyous. Other times we cut ourselves short and
find reasons to downplay joyous things, not realizing if
we downplay them enough, we start believing nothing
is worth being joyous about.

External situations and happenings can make us laugh,
smile, and feel good about ourselves, and give us reason to celebrate. We may feel happiness as a result.
Joy, however, comes from within.

Joy is a state of being, where external factors play no
role in affecting that state. Joy can be an underlying
state beneath surface emotions. Truly felt, Joy emits
through to the surface – it is incapable of being har-

nessed. It is that which bubbles to the surface because it has nowhere else to go but out - to others, to
places, to things – positively affecting those in prox-
imity to it. Joy encompasses the wealth of the universe and expands all space. Joy lacks density – it
ping pongs around, tickling our auras.

There are so many fascinating aspects about us that
we take for granted. We can start by making a list of
them. Even our seemingly negative points are joyous
topics for they provide us the chance to learn and
grow.

There is a Joy domino effect. Once we find Joy in who
we are, we become joyous. In our Joy, we share Joy
with those around us, and they become Joy. The more
we allow ourselves to experience Joy, we find it easier
to remain or come back to that state. We can learn to
be in Joy with whoever we are at any given moment.
The rest will follow.

Week 25 Reflection Exercise

Consider a recent experience where you felt that you suppressed expressing joy for a situation. What made you suppress the joyful emotion?

Was there a time recently where you dismissed or criticized someone for expressing joy? Why?

Do you believe you are worthy to experience Joy every day?

This week, seek at least 10 items to express joy over. Then do so in your own way – not necessarily needing other people's acceptance or knowledge of your expression, yet allowing yourself to express it. The real treasure is expressing it for you.

Week 25 Affirmation

I am open to expressing Joy in my life.

Week 26
Playing Smart

We all know people (including ourselves) who need to be and strive to be considered smart. Whether it's a topic they know nothing about, an opinion is usually had, voiced with great deduction and confidence, even though it may be supported with very little fact or knowledge.

Most play smart individuals have a need to be seen, a need to feel important. Although our society satirizes ultra smart people, we all know who is intelligent and just how wealthy our lives can be when we apply those smarts really well. Some people playing smart want to be perceived a certain way – placing the power of their own self worth into the hands of those with whom they surround themselves. Our society teaches us to judge seemingly not so smart people as less worthy than ones who are perceived as smart. And no one wants to feel less worthy.

We can play our own type of smart when in conversations. We can admit our own lack of knowledge or interest in the topic and if desired, question more about it to learn. We can steer the conversation to a more palatable topic or take up a different conversation with another individual who also may be lacking current topic knowledge or interest.

When playing smart, sometimes we get lucky and the conversation ends on a high note where we shine seemingly as intellectuals. Other times, we back ourselves into a corner, unprepared to respond to subsequent questions on the topic we broached. In either case, we're limited in our ability to respond just so we could "look good" in front of someone, even if that someone is our own self.

It's ok to acknowledge where our smarts on a specific topic begin and end. It provides a level of understanding from the folks we're spending time with. It also helps us determine what new things we'd like to learn more about. Through this acknowledgement, we open doors to allowing new information to enter rather than feeling as though we need to know all the answers.

Experiences seem to be more pleasurable when we simply play ourselves, as we are, in each moment.

Week 26 Reflection Exercise

Can you think upon a time where you acted like you knew something when you really didn't?   How did it make you feel?

What stopped you from being honest and acknowledging outwardly what you didn't know?

Currently are you ok with telling someone you don't know an answer – regardless of topic and your supposed expertise on the topic?

This week, find moments where you are honest with yourself and others about the amount of knowledge you have. It may turn into a great learning experience and prompt some exploration.

Week 26 Affirmation

I am smart and knowledgeable about many things. I acknowledge the topics of which I am less knowledgeable.

Week 27
Applying a Patch

There are patches for clothes, patches applied to software; we grow a patch of grass, put a patch over a cut or wound or a hole in the wall.

Sometimes we automatically judge a situation negatively when that situation requires a patch. The neat thing about patches is they get whatever we're working with from one place to the next. We progress forward by using patches of all kinds.

Patches have wonderful purposes - they can help things heal; they can make a piece of clothing usable again; they can fix a software program error or even add new features to it.

When dealing with others and ourselves we take the time to consider and use patches (emotional, mental, spiritual, or physical) because we know they generate progress. Patches may be discarded after they are used, they can dissolve on their own or they may even become assimilated into the overall product – becoming part of the bigger piece. A new idea, a new emotion – all become part of the bigger whole.

As we work with patches, we learn, individually and collectively, when to keep applying patches or when to take a step back and redesign.

Week 27 Reflection Exercise

Think recently to a time where you felt a need to patch something up – physically or personally. What did you use or how did you go about doing so?

In retrospect, was it successful?

If you have a "next time" to patch up the same or similar aspect again – what would you do differently? Would you employ more help from others?

If the situation was deemed successful and even if it was not, congratulate yourself on having the courage and ideas to patch or attempt to make a patch.

Week 27 Affirmation

I apply patches in my life successfully and accurately. I learn from these experiences, as do those around me.

Week 28
Making the Jump

When we see people bungee jumping, skydiving, ski jumping, or performing a field high jump, obviously, they have all consciously decided to jump. Some folks take time to train for the jump - learning different dynamics, physics, challenges, and joys of the jump. Other folks decide it's an all or nothing kind of a thing with minimal to no training involved.

Regardless how a person chooses to make their jumps in whatever activity they participate in, the common theme of enjoyment is the rush of falling – the rush of the hang time – enjoying the height and feeling exhilarated from it. The momentum of the moment – on all levels - carries them through the event and inspires them to jump again.

Whether we choose to start training with small jumps or with the high jumps, it doesn't matter – one is certainly not better than the other. Any major leaps we feel we need to take in life may require contemplation and preparation, or they may be spur of the moment jumps. Regardless how we determine the leaps we take in our lives, we need to trust ourselves and the experience, savor the hang time, the perspective, and do

our best to carry that exhilarating feeling throughout
our days.

Week 28 Reflection Exercise

What was the most recent experience you partici-
pated in that had you enjoying life for an extended
period of time? This experience may be something
you've thought about quite often since it's occurred or
have spent a lot of time trying to plan another such
occurrence.

Do you look for moments throughout your day to help
recreate that feeling or do you wait until the weekends or your "spare time" to do so? Do you allow yourself that time to experience?

Are there other simpler, everyday moments that you
might perceive with an open heart so you may experience the exhilaration more consistently? What trac-
es of the feeling can you find throughout your week to
carry you through?

What jumps in your life are you considering making?
Are you adequately prepared to make the jump or are
you in the process of deciding?

This week, take some steps to recreate or plan an
event that will generate the same consumption and eu-
phoria.

Week 28 Affirmation

I consistently create inspiring experiences that carry me to growth and success.

Week 29
Blowing the Whistle

Blowing the whistle normally means exposing someone or some act to others who may not be aware of what's going on. If we work with that perspective, blowing the whistle on ourselves helps bring us to being accountable for our actions. By being aware of what we're doing, why we're doing it, and how we can make ourselves different spiritually, we become our own referee, constantly watching, aware, and bringing attention to the things that are against our new rules of living. Except here, there are no penalties. We accept the acknowledgement of the "foul", readjust, and move on.

In the context of self-improvement, we could start with blowing the whistle on ourselves. So when we see that we're doing something – a same limited pattern of thinking or reacting that we're trying to change - we immediately blow the whistle on ourselves. We stop what we're doing, consciously change our behavior or thought process and move on. It may take a few seconds; it may take several minutes and even longer.

From another perspective, blowing the whistle can also be that we need a break – a time out – the whistle signifying half time in the game. We take this time to regroup and see what else we can do. Sometimes it may make sense to sit out the next quarter or half, being supportive, but not necessarily participating actively.

We can be on the lookout for times to blow the whistle on ourselves; determining when we can change the play right then and there or when we need to remove ourselves from the situation – meditate, go for a walk, call a friend, listen to loud music, whatever.

Finally, there's the Whistle of Joy – knowing when to acknowledge our accomplishments and celebrate with music, dance, and song. Blow this whistle to express our happiness in a moment, and allow it to accompany us to the next.

Week 29 Reflection Exercise
When was the last time you noted that someone wasn't doing something "right" or "ethical" according to your judgment or standards?

Did you notice how easy it was to perceive that situation?

When in the past week were you able to view an action you did as "not quite right" or "unethical"? Were you able to see this situation objectively?

Take some time this week to note some of your motives. Are your situations telling you to act or perceive differently, take a break, or celebrate?

Week 29 Affirmation
I am consistently progressing forward with my interpersonal growth.

Week 30
Threading the Needle

Sewing is a beautiful way to create something new, to experiment in expressing who we are. We have a variety of colors and patterns at our fingertips. Lots of us rarely sew except for when we need to thread a needle to sew a button back onto a shirt or mend a small tear in a piece of clothing.

When threading a needle, we need to make sure we choose a needle whose head allows enough space for the thread to pass through. Threading a needle requires focus, steady hands and eventually, a sense for knowing where the two are visually. Experienced sewers have a knack for threading a needle quickly.

There are many times we go through experiences with not enough focus, patience or steadiness and we miss our mark. We may realize that we've missed it right away and we're able to regroup and try again. Other times we don't realize we've missed the needle until we let go of the situation.

Threading a needle requires a relaxed, focused awareness, as do all of life's situations. We require an awareness of our own thoughts and feelings as we move through a situation, as well as an awareness and openness to others' involvement.

If we allow ourselves the time to be that open in all situations – family, work, etc. – we start to see how everything fits together and our situations flow from one to the next with less struggle and intensity.

Initially, maintaining this relaxed, focused awareness can be tiring until our mind and spirit grow accustomed to it. Soon, though, maintaining this relaxed focused awareness becomes second nature to us, just as experienced sewers master the art of threading a needle.

Week 30 Reflection Exercise

Consider an important event or situation playing out in your life right now. Are you paying attention to all the thoughts and emotions that arise during the situation?

Have you taken time to truly feel how it's evolving, and how you fit into the equation?

Consider now an event that you consider less important – perhaps one with family or a friend. Are you taking note of each thought and emotion that arises for this situation? If not, how would this situation play out differently if you were giving it more attention in your own mind and heart?

This week, be careful about the things we swiftly deem as unimportant versus those we place great importance on. The same awareness could be equally valuable in both situations.

Week 30 Affirmation

I pay attention to the nudges of my emotions and thoughts to guide my life in the direction of my heart.

Week 31
Being a Snowflake

Science teaches us that no two snowflakes are exactly alike. They all take minor or major differences in their crystalline form when gently falling from the sky.

Those who watch snowfalls cannot tell from near or far that the snowflakes are different. Each snowflake's uniqueness mostly goes unnoticed. We usually perceive the collective falling of snowflakes rather than taking notice of each distinctive snowflake. Yet, it seems the snowflakes don't seem to mind that we do not notice each of them individually. They fall anyway, possibly proud to be part of the beauty of nature, not worrying about when they will melt or how long they will stay snow. They fall, purely accepting of the moment and being in joy with the part they're playing.

Like snowflakes, humanity is filled with completely different and unique individuals when we look up close physically. We have different nationalities, thought processes, habits, choices, food preferences, etc. We are completely different from each other. Yet from near and far we really are all the same. We all have feelings, insecurities, strengths, and areas of improvements. We have suggestions, opinions, and a heart full of ideas and hope.

The neat thing about snowflakes is they have the opportunity to witness the beauty of all they're creating as they fall from the sky. I like to think when they reach the earth they revel in the joy of being part of such a spectacular, peaceful, wonderful sight.

We too can learn to be more like the amazing snowflake. We can view situations from a higher perspective rather than judging them with our personal tunnel vision within the moment. We can choose to witness the beauty of everything around us realizing that there is more to the scenery than what we may be privy to seeing. We can revel in the joy of being part of everything we are and do today.

Week 31 Reflection Exercise

When was the last time you viewed your family, work group, or other organization of people with a big picture perspective? Just as watching a landscape fill with snow, we can see groups we associate with as big picture landscapes.

Take a few moments and visualize the big picture – the oneness of each group, despite the individuals. Try to see the whole sum of people rather than selecting out the few strong or weak, or annoying individuals. See how the beauty in each shines in their own light.

This week, if you catch yourself judging where you are, who you're with, etc., guide yourself to take a step back and see the bigger picture occurring at that moment. Find the uniqueness of each situation, embracing the individual newness in an ordinary or not so ordinary moment.

Week 31 Affirmation

Today I am less judgmental then yesterday and tomorrow I will be even less judgmental.

Week 32
Shimmering

Shimmering – even the word itself exudes a tender, cool, but just the right warm undertone to it - a soft shine with a wavering, flickering light. Moving but stationery, we find ourselves drawn to it, watching for the shimmer again.

We see shimmers of Light in the darkness. We see shimmers of Light in our family and friends and co-workers. We see shimmers of Light in ourselves. When we see a shimmer of Light, we usually gaze upon the spot where we saw the shimmer in the hopes of seeing it again. We wait for it. We watch for it. We seek it.

When an individual shows a shimmer of a characteristic they may normally not exude, we are struck by it. It catches our attention and we pause, almost seeking it out again. We do the same thing with ourselves. When we see a shimmer of something within us, we may at first be proud and excited or uncertain and confused. We may watch carefully for it again. Or we stop ourselves from letting it out.

Our own shimmers of Light enable us to realize there is more to us than we have yet to explore. When we understand that there is much we have to learn about ourselves, the shimmers no longer frighten us. We're able to turn the shimmer into a shine. And usually, we're happy to have done so.

We can do the same for others too. When we see a shimmer in someone, they may not even be aware of their glow, or they are aware and aren't sure what to do with it. By showing support, we can provide them the encouragement to explore that shimmer further.

At times, we may be inclined to ignore our shimmers or someone else's. Know that if we choose to do that it will eventually come back again. We cannot keep out our Light for that is our purpose – to shimmer our way into shining our Light brightly.

Week 32 Reflection Exercise

Consider a moment recently where you saw a shimmer in someone who you least expected to. What were your initial thoughts?

Consider a recent moment where you saw or felt a shimmer of light within yourself – or maybe someone else noticed and told you about it. Did this excite you or frighten you? Why?

How can you develop this shimmer of light within yourself? How can you nurture it?

How can you do the same for others when you see it sparkling at the most unexpected times? How can you call upon it to inspire?

This week, take one step, regardless how small, to nurturing, celebrating, and developing a shimmer of light that you wish to acknowledge and grow within you.

Week 32 Affirmation

I look for and nurture the light within me and within others.

Week 33
Rounding the Curve

Life throws us many curves. Some are seemingly small curves - some are pretty big curves. Others seem big at first and then we find that they're really small curves and vice versa. How we react to the given life situations certainly varies with whatever state of mind we find ourselves in.

We may not always believe this but we can also determine how quickly or how leisurely we take our turns in life - whether we rush to finish our curves, or meticulously experience each curve to the point it stops our flow. Then there are curves that we savor or pace ourselves by what feels right and what we're comfortable with. We learn when taking the curve feels too fast, or too slow or too intense - and we figure out when it feels smooth, exhilarating, or just a bit challenging or even relaxing. Knowing we have a say in the speed in which we travel our curves, makes them less threatening.

We also know that we can pull off to the side of the road to recoup and gather more of whatever we need before we continue rounding that curve - or when it's time to find a straighter road.

Week 33 Reflection Exercise

Life certainly gives us many twists and turns to work
with and experience. Think of an event or circumstance in your life where you felt life threw you a
curve. Was this a curve that you could have prepared
for or avoided, or one that came across without any
warning?

How do you think you handled the circumstance? Did
you take enough time to sift through all the thoughts
and emotions of the experience? Did you take too
much time overanalyzing things?

Which situations are you currently going through
swiftly and which ones are you taking more cautiously?

This week, take a few moments to verify the pace at
which you're moving in highlights of your life. Can you
comfortably change the pace of any of them? There
is no right or wrong answer, simply what feels right in
your heart.

Week 33 Affirmation

I move comfortably through life's challenges at my
own pace.

Week 34
Walking the Line

Throughout our days, we walk the line of whether to speak and act professionally or with compassion and tact versus how and what we really want to say. We walk the line of social mores and acceptable fashions or behaviors. We also walk the line when we determine whether to share our beliefs on certain topics such as religion and politics. Some people are ready to hear our truth and others are not. Some of us are ready to speak our truth and some of us are not.

Walking the line means being comfortable with our own representation of ourselves versus that which others perceive as acceptable of us.

We often toe the line of our expression of truth and what we perceive others' perception of our expression of truth to be. We block ourselves from the immersion process of a situation for fear of offending others or for fear of rejection by others.

Some of us are comfortable with where those lines exist and have tested the boundaries enough to know when the lines infringe upon our own inner truth - the heart of our beings. It may be time to find other circumstances or perhaps another outlet for us to express our being in its full truth. The more comfortable we are with expressing our full truth, the more inclined we are to find our path and service in this world.

Walking the line of our truth is walking our path - following the perfect guidance of our hearts - not allowing ourselves to be led astray by appearances or other people's influence. We've set this path before us - to walk our path, to toe that line, and shine brighter by walking it.

Week 34 Reflection Exercise

Some days we are met with challenges as the boundaries of our self expression and self sharing change based on our moods, thoughts, conversations, people we meet, expectations we have, and expectations others have. In the past month or so, when have you felt that you were overstepping or under-stepping the boundaries of sharing who you are with others?

Are you able to read when people are prepared for your words, thoughts, and passion, and when they are not? If not, how can you test the waters more easily prior to taking that step? What are some cues that you've experienced in the past?

Know that everyone is different, and sometimes past experience doesn't always help the present. Sometimes you will also simply "know" when to cross that vague line and when not to.

Trust your intuition this week on walking the line of your truth. Silence can be a wonderful way to walk that line as well.

Week 34 Affirmation

I know when to share my truth with others.

Sharing with My Brothers and Sisters

There are many reasons why we choose to share with others. We may choose to share because we think it's the right thing to do, or because it's expected of us, or it makes us look good.

Our hearts, though, want us to truly share our lives with one another – in great excitement. Many of us choose not to share for fear of letting people know who we really are, or to limit others' reactions. We have many reasons that keep us from opening our hearts wide enough to share with great innocence and joy and without any attachments. Many times we put on a front of fake modesty for the sake (or so we think) of others. Other times, we're bubbling with excitement and can't possibly wait to share our news or experience with someone and this is truly elating.

This heartfelt sharing touches people's lives – even if those involved don't realize it. We can create a magnificent world through sharing our lives and ourselves with others.

Week 35 Reflection Exercise

For many of us, we find it quite simple to share – we know who we can share our life trials and joys with and feel utterly comfortable doing so. Take a few moments and revel in the times you have shared accomplishments, goals, etc., with others.

Now take a moment and think of a time where you didn't share your thoughts, experiences, and joys. Why didn't you? How did it feel? Were you being too selective with whom to share?

This week, experiment with sharing levels. We all realize there are people who we share things at different levels. Using your intuition and courage, see if you can increase the levels of sharing or the number of times you share with others. See how this makes you feel. Also, see how this sharing may help others open up to share with you in return.

Week 35 Affirmation

I am a sharing person.

Week 36
Capturing your Audience

As part of everyday lives, we are teaching others through our mere existence and equally learning from others through their existence. We are here for each other yet for ourselves. The lessons we learn are not always in our face, but graze the line of subtlety, catching our attention even if for a brief moment before we move our attention to something else.

We note the difference between mental attention and heart attention. Whatever makes our heart sing is that which catches our heart's attention – not necessarily our mind's attention. By latching on to what our heart desires ensures tremendous growth. We then focus our attention on doing what makes our heart sing – what captivate us. We then become our own captive audience, and even captivate the periodic attention of those around us to the extent they allow.

Our lives prosper when we've captured our own attention – when we become aware of who we want to be and flow from one moment to the next to get there, not even realizing we are captivated by each moment we created.

Week 36 Reflection Exercise

Think about a project you're working on that you think about constantly. You have ideas on how the project should be completed and what it will look like when it's done. Make a list of the thoughts that arise when you think of the project. These items can be general or specific.

Now, take a few moments and breathe deeply. Give yourself time to get centered. Feel or ask the mental body to ease into alignment with the rest of your body. Allow the breath to flow effortlessly throughout your body and your aura.

When you're ready, take some time to feel the emotions behind the thoughts of the project you're working on. Find your breath and that evenness of your mental, emotional, and physical bodies. Allow your heart to fill with the emotions of the project. If you feel joy and warmth – then this project is one that will nourish your heart. If you feel malaise and pressure, see if that's your mind putting more importance on the accomplishment versus enjoying the process.

Through allowing the mind to relax and letting the heart speak, we become more aware and aligned with what brings us joy.

Week 36 – Affirmation

I listen to my heart so I may bring joy and growth into my life.

Week 37
Save Yourself

Many of us are programmed to look for outside sources to save ourselves. Part of society looks toward religion, self-image, possessions, and spiritual teachers and healers to help save us. The bottom line is no one can do the saving for us. Jesus can't save us; Buddha can't save us, etc. Only we can save ourselves.

But what does needing to be saved even mean? Some folks believe that we are inherently bad people and need to be "saved" in order to go to heaven. Others believe that we need to save ourselves from ourselves because we are so spiritually confused; still others believe needing to be saved is a distraction to keep us from remembering that we really don't need to be saved.

We can come up with many aspects of our society, personalities, etc., that could be perceived as needing to be saved – corruption, societal structure, earth pollution, unfair judicial and governmental systems, etc. We may feel we need to save ourselves from our own illnesses, or pain and suffering, individually and collectively. Could it be all we need is change, rather than needing to be saved?

We have the power within ourselves to change our mindsets - to understand and feel what is in our highest potential, our highest good. Our thoughts manifest at great speed. So it's important to focus our minds and hearts.

Let us take a step towards optimism, higher consciousness and save ourselves. Or more accurately, purge our destructive thoughts and actions – to ourselves and others – and replace them with loving and compassionate thoughts and actions. Let's live in a world that no longer needs saving.

Week 37 Reflection Exercise

If there was a specific belief that you grew up with surrounding the thought of needing to be saved, what was it?

What do you believe now about needing to be saved? Has the belief changed over time?

If you have used this book in the order in which it was laid out - what changes have you seen in your world based on any shifts in your perception?

Take a few moments, if you like, and visualize what a perfect world looks like to you. What do cities look like? How are communities structured? How does it feel?

Week 37 Affirmation

I take responsibility for my thoughts and expectations as they pertain to my life and my views of society.

Week 38
Savoring the Lollipop

It's fun to watch children lick those huge lollipops
that are almost as big as their faces – that first lick,
excited for that sweet taste and subsequent ones
where they know they just want more. Eventually,
they find an edge where they attach their mouths until they are able to bite off a chunk. Then, possibly
after multiple bites, through sheer tiredness or over-
saturation, the child chooses to stop eating the taffy
and finds something else to focus on.

Like the child with the lollipop, when the situation is in
front of us looks promising, we excitedly sink our
taste buds into the meat of the experience. If we like
the taste of the situation, we can move ourselves further into the experience to the point where we satu-
rate ourselves. When appropriate, we remove ourselves from the situation and let time pass before we
enter in again, or perhaps choose a different flavor
for next time.

As a society, we become used to saturating our lives
with that which we desire. Sometimes economic features assist us in experiencing a specific flavor of life

more infrequently, while other situations allow us full saturation until the flavor is numb to our taste buds.

There are times that call for saturation with a certain flavor of life, and other times when we benefit from periodically exposing ourselves to another flavor in life.

The balance of saturation and periodic exposure to various flavors in life is our choice to make. Choose wisely, choose freely, and savor each taste.

Week 38 Reflection Exercise

When was the last time you let yourself savor an experience completely? Are you planning for another event or experience where you can allow yourself to be fully saturated by it?

Are you permitting yourself to enjoy enough flavors and variances of experiences, or do you feel that you may be in a rut?

What new flavor or experience are you willing to try next? Is it time to settle back into a routine or comfort level before heading out for a new experience?

Week 38 Affirmation

I allow myself the opportunity to participate in a variety of experiences.

Week 39
Soaring the Skies

Many of us attempt to know what it feels like to soar the skies, literally. Through sky diving, bungee jumping, floating in hot air balloons, or hang gliding, many of us obtain a certain "high" from experiencing such heights.

Even the more grounded folk find ways to get the same high – through running, sports, or elation and excitement after meditation, or spring fever, etc. As we grow, we learn more about what aspects of life's participation provide us with that natural high. Is it a conversation about a specific topic? Is it an activity, or even a non-activity?

Sometimes we forget to take the time to explore what gives us that high. Sometimes we allow ourselves to stumble across that elating experience. We remove ourselves from the daily grind, see things with a new perspective and slowly, we learn what inspires our feelings.

Soaring the skies enables us to be closer with our spiritual selves, and provides our Spirit with a sense of home, safety, confidence, and a higher state of mind.

Our task here on earth may be to find those things that make us soar, partake in them often, and remembering to leave room for even better and more soaring opportunities to enter our lives.

Week 39 Reflection Exercise

What activities do you regularly do that make your heart sing or keep you figuratively walking on air for days afterwards?

Do you make these activities a part of your regularly scheduled program? Are you able to successfully carry over the feeling into the perceived "drab" areas of your life?

What can you do to experience soaring-type experiences more often?

How can you include others in those experiences as well?

Week 39 Affirmation

I am open to exhilarating experiences.

Week 40
Singing in a Choir

When we join a choir, depending on the pitch of our voice, we are placed into a specific section -sopranos, tenors, altos, etc. - knowing our voice will help develop the beauty of the songs and perhaps touch whoever chooses to listen. Most successful choirs have individuals who are committed to their participation. They rehearse individually and collectively. They work together to have their melody sounding as best as possible.

While singing in the choir, we may not realize how we sound to the audience. We assume or take for granted that we sound ok or good. Stepping outside of the choir and listening to the song as a spectator takes on a whole new perspective. We begin to hear things we ordinarily would not have heard while being in the choir. We may tune into sounds that may need improvement or we may realize that the sound touches our hearts more than anticipated. Either way, when it's time to return to singing in the choir, we resume our position with a newfound appreciation and inspiration of our mission.

In life situations, it's beneficial to immerse ourselves in our experiences – learning and rehearsing on our own and playing well with others. When it feels time, there is much value in taking a step away and watching the situation as a spectator would. Stepping outside of the situation and viewing it as a spectator would, provides a great opportunity to objectively view a situation and determine how we may like to change it, if at all.

Since we've broadened our perception of the experience by stepping outside it, we have the space and freedom to grow more fully into or because of that situation.

Week 40 Reflection Exercise

Ponder a situation that you're really involved in. It can be a project, a situation with a relationship or an evaluation of our own reactions to something.

What aspects of the situation are going well? Which could be going better?

You may feel compelled to see the situation from all sides possible to get a full spectrum of perspectives. Let's take it a bit further and view the situation from a bird's eye perspective – with complete objectivity. Now what do you see?

In this light, are there any constructive criticisms that you did not see before? Are there any constructive criticisms that can be omitted from this view?

Week 40 Affirmation

I am readily able to recognize areas of improvement and acknowledge when things are going well.

Standing in Line

Whether we're out shopping or paying a toll on the interstate, many of us quickly scope out the options prior to committing to waiting in a specific line. We try to get in what we perceive as the shortest line. Many of us grow quite annoyed to wait in a line, especially if we're in a rush to get somewhere. Many of us also grow irritated with waiting in line even when we have no specific timeframes to meet. While it's true that we've created such busy schedules for ourselves, waiting in line is a time commodity that we simply deem unacceptable or inappropriate.

For our mental mind, standing in line signifies a lull or stop or decrease in progress. We're not getting through to our destination fast enough. We've been programmed to believe that not progressing forward all the time is detrimental to the end result. Yes, lines do create a break in the physical progress of moving from one place to another. As such, they can easily provide a mental break as well. Since we are not moving as fast as we'd like or had expected, this lack of physical forward movement gives us a chance to slow our minds down, if we allow it to. We can take a few minutes to stand and breathe deeply, or maybe even chat with those around us.

When standing in line, there is always the option to change lines or step out of the line altogether. Given our timeframes or our current desires at the moment, is this line truly in our best interest to wait in? Whether it's a line for a promotion, a new stage in a relationship, or that perfect home – is it truly in our best interest to stand here? Or is it time for us to change lines or drop out of line altogether?

Only we know our heart's desire, our personal limitations, our own challenges, and our own divine plan. We are in charge of us. What lines will we choose to step into and wait regardless of time? What lines will we choose to change or remove our participation in?

Week 41 Reflection Exercise

How do you respond to waiting when you know you're going to be doing so – whether in a doctor's office, or an airport, etc.?

How do you respond when you aren't expecting a wait and are faced with one?

What figurative lines have you been standing in for what you perceive as too long? Do you make others wait?

Is there something you can do to pass the time more quickly while you wait? Or is it time to re-evaluate what you're waiting for and your options to achieve that something?

Week 41 Affirmation

I carefully and respectfully choose the lines I stand in. I am a patient and discerning person.

Week 42
Glazing a Donut

Glazing a donut is finding a small thing to be grateful for - a sweet, loved item or aspect, and finding that little detail that makes it even more appreciated. Throughout the day we notice lots of blessings, many of which we may take for granted. By thinking thoughts of gratitude for the relatively small things in life that we assume and expect, makes those items glisten in our hearts.

For example, take a spectacular building with interesting or innovative architecture for its time. Most people will view that building with awe and wonder at its shape or size, acknowledging that it is a grand piece of architecture. Yet some folks will take the time to study the ingenuity of each stage of building the structure. Even others will admire the texture of the materials used and how the structure was secured. Each detail of that building is appreciated in addition to its whole being acknowledged. As a whole, that structure is appreciated, yet people find different aspects within that whole to be equally appreciated, if not more so.

There are aspects within each of us that deserve detailing and highlighting as an honored portion of the whole. There are those aspects within all of us – within all things – concrete and abstract. What will you find in the details to appreciate, honor, and celebrate today?

Week 42 Reflection Exercise

Take a few moments to write down the many positive aspects of yourself. If you need help coming up with a list of things, ask family and friends what they perceive as your positive traits.

Take each aspect or characteristic about you and write next to it a way in which you can celebrate and honor that part of you.

For each day this week, take one or two (or more, if applicable) of the aspects, and partake in the celebratory activity you noted above.

Each day, be aware of your own reaction to yourself, and others' reactions to your celebration - even those who are unaware of what you're focusing on.

Week 42 Affirmation

I am a wonderful being. I take time to celebrate and honor myself for who I am.

Week 43
Fitting the Glove

Many of us aspire to fulfill a purpose in this world – to make a contribution or even strive to be remembered. We try our hand at many different skills, jobs, and relationships. We learn where we fit in the best, where we need improvement, and where we really lack a knack for something.

Sometimes we think we know what we want and when we get there, we realize it doesn't quite fit us the way we thought it would. In doing so, we learn what we like, what we don't like, what we want most and what we need. We learn how to deal with others, and most importantly, how to deal with ourselves.

Other times we're in a situation that suits us just fine but we may not even realize it until we move to another place or situation. That's a-okay too for we can draw on what the previous situation felt like and recreate it for our new endeavors.

Throughout our experiences, we've worn loose fitting gloves that we had to grow into; tight gloves, that we needed to let go of; and gloves that fit perfectly, even if temporarily. We know that situations will ebb and flow with our own growth and various factors. With awareness, we can choose to embrace the current set of gloves we wear or change gloves when we need to. It's important to have fun with each pair; being who we are in each moment, regardless what our gloves say about us or have us doing.

Week 43 Reflection Exercise

Think back over the past five or ten years of your life. Which situations along the way did you outgrow, or grow into, or slide right into perfectly?

In the past, have you always known when it's time to switch gloves, or hang onto them so you can grow a little more?

Have you spent a lot of time in challenging situations or easy ones? When the challenging situations came, did you quickly find easier ones to replace them or did you continue full steam ahead?

As you go about your week, be aware of the situations you're in which seem challenging. They may be the opportunities for you to grow into oversized gloves, or they could be you outgrowing your current gloves.

Spend some time determining what you want from each situation and see if there is any need to change where you are, where you're going, or if it's a matter of changing your perception along the way.

Week 43 Affirmation

I am open to facing challenges that help me grow.

Week 44
Loving the Glove

Inevitably, we, or some spectator, will comment or judge the pair of gloves we're wearing. Someone or we may say what we're doing doesn't fit us well; that our current gloves are too colorful, too big, small, or just not a good representation of us. Once we think our gloves are faulty we put the energy out there for new ones. And then we see it - a glove that is more appealing to us - one that leads us to dislike our current glove or judge it less.

There is great importance in expressing daily gratitude for the current gloves we wear. Only we know if and when it's time to find another glove that suits our liking just fine.

It may be helpful, though, to check out that glove we find more appealing – study it, try it on and see if it provides the same comforts as our current gloves. Does it stretch our comfort zone or does it constrict our ability to move? In exploring the seemingly more appealing glove, we may find our current glove is simply fine and maybe we'd been taking too much for granted.

We may choose to keep our current gloves for the rest of our lives here. We may have the opportunity to change them often. As long as our hearts our open with the greatest of Love, all our gloves can be cherished for their unique traits and characteristics.

By loving our current gloves, our current life situation, we keep our hearts open to the opportunities of more abundant life situations or new gloves, as appropriate. When we focus on the negatives of our current gloves, we wallow in that place, attracting more of that in which we wallow, keeping any new opportunities away.

Loving where we are in every moment can seem challenging at times. With diligent and sometimes, not so deep attention to the reasons for discomfort, we open ourselves up to the items we can perceive differently, and take charge of the aspects we can change on our own and the gloves acquired or maintained in that space.

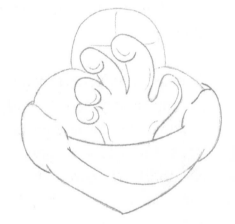

Week 44 Reflection Exercise

Identify a current situation in your life that you take for granted.

What does this situation provide for you?

Take a few moments and sit in gratitude for all this situation offers you.

This week, when you find yourself dreading an activity or aspect or situation, attempt to take some time to sit back and reflect upon what the situation is giving you. It could be a material aspect or a personal characteristic/perspective that's being developed.

Week 44 Affirmation

I keep my heart open and am I need to be at all times.

Week 45

Order vs. Chaos

Both can trigger progress. Without one, we cannot have the other. There is a distinct need, time and place for order to be prevalent, and there is also great productivity in the art of chaos.

For some, chaos brings great turmoil and insecurity. Fear is readily present. However, within chaos, we can find productivity and safety if we allow ourselves time to explore and seek it out.

Eventually, chaos brings about some type of order. And in time, order eventually stokes some amount of chaos. Both bring about change. Both bring about solidarity of like minds and like hearts. That's why there are different organizations, sports, political parties, activist groups, etc., working towards some common purpose. Some people work to provide order for what are perceived as chaotic people or situations. Others work to break down a system and promote a healthy chaos in the search for change.

Judge not whether one is better than the other. Seek the value of order and chaos in each situation, and attempt to find the solace in each.

Week 45 Reflection Exercise

Consider a portion of your life that you view as being in perfect order.

Consider a portion of your life that you view as being in chaos.

List out some pros and cons for each item above. What do you like about each? What do you dislike about each?

What is each situation cultivating in you? What are you cultivating to each situation?

This week, as you are confronted with orderly and chaotic aspects of life, determine if they truly are orderly or chaotic. Can the orderly situations use a dose of chaos? Or can the chaotic ones use a dose of order? Or are they moving along just fine as they are?

Week 45 Affirmation

I seek out the benefit of chaos and order in a healthy balance.

Week 46
Touching Ground

Just like a breath of fresh air after being inside a closed building, or underwater for a couple seconds too long, touching ground after soaring the skies can be a relieving and welcoming sensation. We feel "normal" again yet, we may worry how long we'll need to wait for a situation that provides that "high" again – or we immediately start to plan another event in the hopes that elation will return.

What we sometimes forget is that we need to touch ground regularly. It's like exercise - after we exercise, we need to give our muscles rest before exercising again (decreasing the chance for soreness or injury). Rest is an important part of the exercise cycle. It provides time for our muscles to recover, grow, and our metabolism to burn.

After our soaring experiences, our Spirit also needs some down time, some time to regroup and rest. All our bodies - our physical, emotional, mental, and spiritual bodies – need to recover from the experience and integrate the experience to grow. We provide our Spirits some time to rest so we can experience the next moment to its fullest.

We also need to touch ground so others can be affected by our energy in between the highs. This energy can be relaxing; it can be rejuvenating or inspiring. It can bring warmth and hope to others, or a reason for people to smile. Regardless, we have the power to touch other's lives by living ours.

Week 46 Reflection Exercise

Remember a time after a soaring experience – maybe a day or two later. Did you still have remnants of the inspiration and exhilaration inside?

Were you excited yet drained from the experience? How did you feel after you rested from the experience?

Were others able to tell that you had just experienced something very neat from your perspective?

This week, notice any soaring experiences you may have. Remember to allow yourself the time to integrate the experience, which may mean rest or sharing with others. Realize that however you feel, because you have raised your own vibration, your presence is affecting others to raise theirs. See if you can notice any obvious influence in others while you're planning/ waiting for the next soaring experience.

Week 46 Affirmation

I effortlessly transition to and from soaring experiences.

Week 47
Stoking the Fire

Sometimes it feels as though we have so much going on – that all our dreams or desires are coming to fruition and we barely have the time to notice and appreciate all that is happening. There also may come a cycle where all the excitement ends or there doesn't seem to be anything happening – no sparks of inspiration, no great joys, and a seeming lack of motivation. These are the times we must take personal inventory and discern if the universe is providing us with a much needed resting period or if we need to do something to break free of the energetic rut.

There are lots of times when we get ourselves caught up in the seeming monotony of our lives or what we feel we need to do. We can learn to recognize when we're in these phases, and help ourselves get out of them. We can switch up our routine; we can take a day for ourselves; we can do something we love to do even if it means spending a little extra money; we can call a friend for a pick me up or watch a funny movie. It's all about finding ways to inspire ourselves.

Realize that we may need to jolt our systems a bit – try a different approach or muster up some willpower and openness to be inspired.

To stoke our own fires, we must be willing to move the logs around or add some kindling so the fire can burn strongly again when the flames grow dim. And of equal importance we must learn to read when the dim flame is the calm before catching a spark versus a dim flame on its way out. We may need to work a little at finding the sparks of inspiration and motivation in our lives.

Week 47 Reflection Exercise

Think of a moment in the past six months where you felt as though you had nothing going on, weren't inspired, or had little motivation to do anything to reach your goals.

Were there ways in which you could have sparked an inspiration somehow? Or was this needed downtime?

Sometimes it's easy to say downtime is always needed, for that is a very important part of our lives. However, next time you find yourself in the uninspired state, attempt to inspire yourself.

Write some inspiring options for yourself to try so you have a reference. Make them attainable. Place this list on your refrigerator or nightstand – somewhere you can see it everyday. You may not wish to wait until you're in an inspirational slump to try some of your suggestions. If you feel so inspired, take a chance to inspire yourself when you're already motivated. That alone could carry you past an inspirational drought without you even realizing.

Week 47 Affirmation

I find intriguing ways to be inspired and balance out the activity with sufficient down time in my life.

Week 48
Filling Another's Cup

Filling another's cup happens when we are open to sharing our true selves with another. It is helpful, but not always necessary, for the person we're sharing with to be consciously receptive to what we have to share.

Through our own personal experiences, we can fill another's cup with hope and joy. We can also fill our cups with qualities such as self-confidence, self-reliance, laughter, connection, acceptance, love, harmony, etc., so much so that these qualities overflow into the cups of those around us. In this way, filling another's cup is always a joyous experience, since we are giving to others that which we already possess in abundance.

We must be careful, though, to be sure we are filling another's cup without draining our own. There comes a point while maintaining responsibility to ourselves, we learn to discern when it is appropriate to step away from an extended cup and allow that person to fill their cup on their own. And we do so with gratitude – gratitude for the person extending their cup, and gratitude towards ourselves for maintaining our own sovereignty and well being.

It's important to discern when to replenish our own cup's supply, so we are more apt and greatly success-fully in filling others' as we move about our day.

We can also realize that sometimes filling another person's cup helps fill ours as well. For example, when we've agreed to do something for another and when the time comes we find we aren't in the best mood to do so, or something happens that dampens our spirits and lessens our energy. Yet, occasionally, when we follow through and do that something, it helps move us into a better place. Our willingness and ability to be there for another, to fill someone else's cup, may in-evitably fill ours as well.

Week 48 Reflection Exercise

Filling another's cup can be as simple as sending a good thought or smile their way or spending time helping or talking with them. A compliment is always a nice place to start.

Can you think of a time or specific person you who you helped along your travels, and then felt drained from the experience?

Do you recall if you were drained before you started helping or as a result from helping?

What ways could you have prepared yourself for the event? What ways could you have altered the event to be more conscious and active of your own energy levels?

Now recall an experience where you helped someone and felt energized by it. How was that circumstance different from the above one? Can you tell the difference of how it felt going into the situation as well as coming out of it? What did you feel was given to you in return?

This week take some time to feel your energy levels before stepping in to help someone else. Are you able to give energy to help but not depleting yours in the process? Are you able to recognize when the experience may help someone AND help you at the same time?

Week 48 Affirmation
I am aware of my state of being especially when I am helping others.

Week 49
Evaluating the Meal

Many societies have become focused on making evaluations on just about everything – apparel, food, job performance, other societies, etc. We have evaluations on consumer products, in social interactions; we over-evaluate a situation, our reactions and other people's participation in a situation. We evaluate food as soon as we see it, and again as soon as it touches our taste buds. By nature, and through practice, humans have become great evaluators.

When we venture out to try a new place to eat or when we're invited over a person's house, we usually take a moment during and after the fact to evaluate the meal or food prepared for the day's events. We note what we liked about the food, what we didn't like, the textures, what dishes and drinks complimented each other. These are all very well used methods of evaluating our meal.

We can apply the same evaluation techniques with life experiences. After the experience is over, we can evaluate how we felt during the entire experience – what portions of the experience lifted our hearts and which ones turned our stomachs or made us feel uncomfortable. We can reason with ourselves as to why we did like certain parts of the experiences versus others and possibly determine where we can improve upon our responses the next time around.

Although we have learned to be great evaluators at heart and know we can learn a lot about ourselves when doing so, we also can learn from deciding when not to evaluate at all; for accepting the moment just as it is and being ok with that; for allowing the moment to pass un-judged, simply being there, aware, and free.

By going back and forth in freedom and evaluation, we find more balance in our lives and more joy in our experiences.

Week 49 Reflection Exercise

Although some of us are great evaluators already we need to also be able to differentiate from over-evaluating and obsessing over something. Evaluation is an objective assessment of the experience based on your expectations, wants, and likes or dislikes, etc. It's the ability to let go of the attachment to the event enough to see how we could do things different-ly, accept what we have control over and what we don't, and allowing others to be who they are.

This week, as we evaluate our experiences, remember to take a look at the seemingly small happenings that cause big or surprising emotional reactions in us. The gift is to work with detaching from the way things should have gone, and open up to how we want things to be from this point, moving forward.

Week 49 Affirmation

I am objective and open to self-improvement. I de-tach easily from the expected outcome and assess my participation in life with objectivity.

Week 50
Flying a Kite

Kites come in varied shapes, sizes and colors. Lots of us will stop and watch a flying kite, enamored by it hovering in the wind, stabled only by a piece of string.

Kites are viewed as relaxing; they signify freedom, flight, an inherent ability to ride the wind, and maintain altitude. To some, they signify skill, creativity, and finesse.

Just like kites, people come in many different shapes, colors, and sizes. To us, catching the wind means riding the upswing of flow in a situation. If our timing and intentions are accurate, we fly high, maintain our height, and good things come to us with great ease. However, not all weather is kite flying weather. On these days we wait patiently or work towards our next kite flying day. And even when it is good kite flying weather, it may take a few tries to catch the wind and raise ourselves up. Persistence and awareness is key.

Kites can stay in one place and soar. We, too, can remain in one place and reach new heights without changing our location. We can shine brightly just where we are.

Week 50 Reflection Exercise

Take a few moments and visualize a kite flying in the wind, hovering, flowing. Now, in your mind's eye merge yourself with that kite and feel what it feels like to be up that high, the wind against your body, seeing the world from a different experience. How does it feel?

Think of an experience where you felt similar feelings. What new experiences can you create to experience those feelings again?

Week 50 Affirmation

I graciously experience the natural highs of life.

Week 51
Enjoying the Dessert

Most of us enjoy indulging in a sweet, tasty treat. We savor the texture of the dessert, the taste of the dessert, and the sensation and emotional enjoyment of it reaching our taste buds. Sometimes we respectfully pause before taking another bite. Despite such an appreciated experience, dessert is something we do not always allow ourselves to partake in – especially the ones we judge as the truly decadent desserts.

The same goes for our lives. Often, we figure on skipping "dessert". In some cases, that means skipping an experience that might bring us much joy, elation, or satisfaction on a heartfelt, innocent level. We may choose to skip the experience because we're too tired, or we've had enough experiences for one day – or in fear that the experience may not be as good as we hope it will be.

Many people can tell us how great a dessert is but we must remember that is their experience. We may not enjoy the same qualities in a dessert that the person next to us does. Going on another person's say so is not always the wisest choice. Many people rave about certain experiences, but when we get there, we may not experience the same level of emotion that someone else did or does.

Clearly, we must listen to ourselves and our hearts, to know when it's right for us to experience a dessert like experience. It may happen in the midst of a busy day at work, or it may be a long weekend planned months in advance.

Dessert may mean skipping an appetizer or even a main course once in a while. Let's allow ourselves the chance to enjoy and immerse ourselves into the full experience of dessert – whether it's a food treat, or a night out with friends, or an entire day off from work alone. Let's allow ourselves to choose our desserts from the heart without judgment, trusting that our bodies will benefit from the sweetness we bring to it.

Week 51 Reflection Exercise

Think of a recent time where you opted to skip having a good time or what you perceived as a good opportunity because of other responsibilities, or the initial thought of "I can't do that".

When was the last time you allowed yourself something fun to do even if for a moment or two – without judgment – a purely innocent moment?

What rules do you have that may be self-created, that restrict you from nurturing yourself with a little fun? Take a few moments to evaluate if these rules still apply for you. Then, ask yourself why they still apply to you?

This week, notice when you are rejecting a fun moment- you know what it feels like – it can be someone trying to make you laugh or your child wanting to play. This week, say yes to a perceived fun invitation when you normally would've said no. How does it feel?

Week 51 Affirmation

I sprinkle my life with healthy doses of fun throughout my days.

Week 52
Fun Times that Last

Most of us like to have fun. We like making plans to
have fun times - we plan family nights, weekends with
friends, and guys' and girls' nights out. At times, we're
disappointed when the good times end. We may be
saddened because we have a mindset of returning to
the mundane and serious and wish there could be more
fun in all of that.

To an extent, we can make it fun. We are able to make
otherwise perceived mundane moments fun. We make
cleaning up fun for kids; in fact, we make lots of
chores fun for kids – why not do the same for ourselves as adults? Can we make a game out of the laundry or doing the dishes or can we simply find solace
and contentment throughout our tasks?

Fun and Joy build each other. When we're in Joy,
we're more open to having and being fun. Sometimes
we need to have fun to realize we feel Joy. And once
in true Joy, the fun times keep coming – full of heart.

Week 52 Reflection Exercise

Reflect back to a time when you were younger. Do you remember making a game out of everything?

As younger kids, even if our chores weren't fun, we rushed through them because we always had something fun to do next - play with neighborhood friends or siblings, make up a new game, play with our toys. It was all about playing. As adults, our play time is greatly decreased, maybe even nonexistent.

This week, consider making games out of tasks at your job, or chores around the house. Make even up a silly jingle to go with your work. Reward yourself with listening to a favorite song or after so many minutes of a specific work task give yourself a treat. Feel free to solicit family members and coworkers to help build more fun in your days.

Week 52 Affirmation

I am a fun person.

Bonus Week
Slowing the Pace

Much of society today is about filling our days with things to do – accomplishing as much as we can in our waking hours. There is so much to learn, so much to see, so much to do, that sometimes we lose sight of the necessity to slow things down a bit – savor each task and accomplishment. We certainly can control the pace at which we work or complete our activities.

It may be seem difficult to slow the pace – but it can be done. We can test the boundaries for ourselves, and see what works for us. Slowing down the pace usually produces higher quality productivity with the proper focus. If we find our days full of appointments and activities, whether for our children, our parents, or ourselves, perform the tasks at a slower pace, en-joying the moments that make up the task, rather than rushing through them.

Slowing the pace brings grace to our presence. We have a handle on being more relaxed as we work, and our bodies - physically, mentally, and emotionally – show it. We move from one task to another with open-ness, purity, and fluidity. Our muscles are no longer tight. Our demeanor becomes more pleasant, and we begin to enjoy moments we previously were too hurried to enjoy. We develop better solutions to issues that may arise; we see the world more clearly.

Slowing the pace allows us to remain focused and open all at once. Our perspectives broaden and our hearts open to more possibilities and more laughter. By slowing down we give ourselves permission to enjoy the sweetness of life.

Bonus Week Reflection Exercise

Think of a time in your recent weeks where you rushed someone or cut someone short because you were in a hurry. Are you typically late to meetings or appointments because you're rushing to get there or get other things done while you're getting there?

Now think of a time in your recent weeks where you took your time doing something. If you cannot think of anything, imagine something that you would enjoy taking your time doing. How did/does it feel?

This week, take some time to notice how often you're rushing and how often you're taking your time. You may even want to keep a tally if you can. Make it point this week, to slow yourself down at least three times. Taking deep breaths will help you slow your pace.

Bonus Week Affirmation

I savor the benefits of taking my time to complete daily tasks.

Bonus Week
Matching Socks

There may come a moment when we find we've mis-
matched a pair of socks that do not match by our
standards. The toe and heel may be reinforced or a
different color on one sock and not the other. One
sock may be longer than the other or a different color
altogether. We can usually tell quite quickly when
we've mistakenly matched socks. Sometimes we find
out after we've reached our destination for the day,
and are unable to head home and change. What is our
normal reaction to this experience? Are we embar-
rassed and hide or quickly go purchase a matching pair
of socks? Or do we laugh and light heartedly enjoy
the quirk of the day?

We may each have our own standards around wearing
matching socks - when it's appropriate to, when it's ok
to mix and match, and when it's not ok to mix and
match. It's purely a subjective perspective based on
our comfort levels, and how seriously we take ourselves. We're all human and the more we level out the
playing field, the more fun it becomes.

For some people, mixing and matching socks will be going out on a limb; other people will find great fun and bask in the attention it brings.

Matching socks may be important in some moments, and invariably inconsequential in others. Where in our lives do we require focus and brevity? Where in our lives could we expand on color and expression and try a new approach? We can practice determining where our comfort level is with maintaining order and matched socks, and where in our lives we can try mixing and matching our experiences, our perspectives, and see what we learn. How does it feel when we mix and match our experiences and perceptions in a given situation? How does it feel when we match?

Bonus Week Reflection Exercise

Consider if people over the course of your life have told you that you take things too seriously.

Now consider if people over the course of your life have commented about how light hearted you are – how you see the brighter side of things and don't get your feathers ruffled very often.

How do you react to social faux pas that you make?

Are you able to admit, accept and laugh about them, or do you shun yourself and accept others' or your own ridicule of you?

It's amazing how people react to things that are "out of place" in their world – ourselves included. Some folks welcome a breath of fresh air – something new. In others, it raises insecurities and they are uncertain of how to act.

This week, take some time to mix and match your perceived socially acceptable behaviors. See which ones feel liberating, and which ones serve a purpose.

At least twice refrain from judging someone else for not complying to a perceived social norm as well.

Bonus Week Affirmation
I am open to new perspectives and new approaches.

About the Author

Pamela Aloia is an energy worker, holding certifications in various energy modalities including Reiki (Master/Teacher), Integrated Energy Therapy, Reflexology, and Magnified Healing. She is also an Associate Certified Coach, with  clients in the pastoral and business arena and has spent a large portion of her life studying martial arts. Pamela enjoys working and growing together with her clients and students, and holds workshops and lectures on meditation, energy work and coaching. Pamela believes in enriching the lives of others through enriching her own and looks forward to all life has to offer. She favors spending time with her family, experiencing the outdoors, exercising regularly, and being open to new opportunities to understand, witness, or participate in the miracles of today. Pamela is also the author of *Nurturing Healthy Change* and coauthor of *Rescuer Mindset*. She has also produced an inspiring meditation CD titled *Channels of Light*.

For more information on Pamela, her workshops, personal consultations, events and publications, visit *www.solangel.com*.